Yale Studies in English

Benjamin Christie Nangle, Editor

Volume 161

"Art-speech is the only truth."

Studies in Classic American Literature, 1923

"What novels we could write, if we wrote of the whole good we knew, instead of the good that may be in this world!"

To Middleton Murry, 1915
D. H. Lawrence: A Composite Biography

"The most interesting figure in modern art is Cézanne: and that not so much because of his achievement as because of his struggle."

"Introduction to These Paintings," 1929

D. H. Lawrence as a Literary Critic

David J. Gordon

New Haven and London / Yale University Press / 1966

Preface

This study began as an examination of an important but neglected aspect of a major writer, and grew more complex as I came to recognize that the theory basic to his literary criticism leads into the general structure of his art and thought. It moves, then, between analysis of specific literary judgments and analysis of such larger topics as art and morality, myth and history, unconscious and conscious mind. Lawrence had a wonderful ability to detect the hidden intentions of "art-speech" and a more problematic ability to shape his insight into a vast moral argument, an argument the more persuasive and difficult to separate from the descriptive content of his criticism because of his formidable moral passion and rhetorical skill. My hope is that this study will not only increase the currency of his many useful and interesting literary judgments but will also shed light on some of Lawrence's general assumptions, which are shared, in large part, by other writers in the Romantic tradition.

The greatest debts I have incurred in preparing this book are to Martin Price, who read the manuscript in its densest state and helped me both to discover my own logic and to develop some implications I had overlooked; and to Harold Bloom, who stimulated my thinking on Lawrence and Romanticism in a variety of ways. I am grateful also to other members of the Yale English Department who made helpful suggestions at different stages of the work: Louis Martz, Charles Feidelson, Norman H. Pearson, R. W. B. Lewis, and Eugene Waith. Finally, I want to thank my editor, Wayland Schmitt, for skillful guidance in matters of presentation.

In its initial form, as a doctoral dissertation presented to the Yale Graduate School, the work received the John Addison Porter Prize in 1961.

New York   D.J.G.
September 1965

Acknowledgments

Quotations from the following works are reprinted by permission of The Viking Press, Inc., and Laurence Pollinger, Ltd.:
Studies in Classic American Literature by D. H. Lawrence. Copyright 1923, 1950 by Frieda Lawrence, © 1961 by the Estate of the late Mrs. Frieda Lawrence. All rights reserved.
"Desire Is Dead," "Tragedy," and "Now It's Happened" from *The Complete Poems of D. H. Lawrence,* Vol. I, and "Red Geranium and Godly Mignonette" from *The Complete Poems of D. H. Lawrence,* Vol. II, edited by Vivian De Sola Pinto and F. Warren Roberts. Copyright 1929 by Frieda Lawrence Ravagli. All rights reserved.
The Symbolic Meaning by D. H. Lawrence, edited by Armin Arnold. Copyright © 1960 by the Estate of the late Mrs. Frieda Lawrence.
The Collected Letters of D. H. Lawrence, edited by Harry T. Moore. Copyright © 1962 by Angelo Ravagli and C. Montague Weekley, Executors of the Estate of Frieda Lawrence Ravagli. All rights reserved.

Quotations from the following copyrighted works are reprinted by permission of William Heinemann, Ltd.:
Phoenix: The Posthumous Papers of D. H. Lawrence, edited by Edward D. McDonald.
The Letters of D. H. Lawrence, edited by Aldous Huxley.

Chapter Four of this book appeared in slightly different form in *Perspective* (Winter 1964) and is reprinted with the permission of its editor, Jarvis Thurston.

Contents

Preface v

Acknowledgments vi

Abbreviations viii

1 Introduction 1

2 The Critic 17

3 The Aesthetic 41

4 The Quarrel with Tragedy 75

5 Myth and History 96

6 Heroes of Death and Heroes of Rebirth 111

7 The Case of Whitman and the Limits of Ideological Criticism 133

8 Conclusion 146

Appendix: An Index to Lawrence's Literary Criticism 153

Bibliography 159

Index 165

Abbreviations

The titles of frequently quoted works by (and in the case of the *Composite Biography*, by and about) Lawrence have been abbreviated as follows:

AA	*Assorted Articles*
Apoc.	*Apocalypse*
"A Propos"	"A Propos of Lady Chatterley's Lover"
CB	*D. H. Lawrence: A Composite Biography*
CL	*The Collected Letters of D. H. Lawrence*
CP	*The Complete Poems of D. H. Lawrence*
F	*Fantasia of the Unconscious*
L	*The Letters of D. H. Lawrence*
P	*Phoenix: The Posthumous Papers of D. H. Lawrence*
PU	*Psychoanalysis and the Unconscious*
R	*Reflections on the Death of a Porcupine and Other Essays*
S	*Studies in Classic American Literature*
SL	*The Selected Letters of D. H. Lawrence*
SM	*The Symbolic Meaning: The Uncollected Versions of Studies in Classic American Literature*
T	*The Tales of D. H. Lawrence*

Because of the numerous editions of the novels, references to them are cited by chapter rather than page.

Full publication information is provided in the Bibliography.

D. H. Lawrence as a Literary Critic

I

Introduction

Lawrence's reputation as a literary critic is still marginal, but his criticism, judged by its quantity, quality, and scope, must rank as a major area of his achievement. It is chiefly represented by *Studies in Classic American Literature;*[1] by *Phoenix: The Posthumous Papers*

1. The work exists in three versions different enough to be worth distinguishing. The essays were originally written in Cornwall in 1917, and eight of them—"The Spirit of Place," "Benjamin Franklin," "Hector St. John de Crèvecoeur," "Fenimore Cooper's Anglo-American Novels," "Fenimore Cooper's Leatherstocking Novels," "Edgar Allan Poe," (part of) "Nathaniel Hawthorne," and "The Two Principles" (a cosmological introduction to Dana and Melville)—were published in *The English Review* from November 1918 to June 1919. These, including the whole of the Hawthorne essay but not the essays on Dana, Melville, and Whitman, which are probably lost, have recently been collected into book form by Armin Arnold, under the title *The Symbolic Meaning* (New York, 1964). They will be called *Studies* I or version I, and will be cited as they appear in book form. Version I was revised in Sicily in 1920, but only one essay of this revision was published, that on Whitman, in *The Nation and The Athenaeum* (July 23, 1921). The essays "Herman Melville's *Typee and Omoo*" and "Herman Melville's *Moby Dick*" had lain in manuscript until they too were collected, along with "Whitman," in *The Symbolic Meaning*. They will be called *Studies* II or version II, and will also be cited as they appear in book form. The familiar *Studies in Classic American Literature* —hereafter called *Studies, Studies* III, or version III—represents an extensive revision, made in America during the winter of 1922–23 and first published in 1923. It gathers together all the essays of versions I and II except "The Two Principles." The edition I will cite is that published by Doubleday Anchor (New York, 1953).

of D. H. Lawrence, that extraordinary anthology of prefaces, reviews, and miscellaneous essays which provides a record of the critic at every stage of his career; and by the voluminous letters, themselves an anthology of vivid critical commentary. Noteworthy criticism can also be found in almost every one of the many books of nonfiction that Lawrence wrote, and in his fiction and verse as well.[2] His primary interests as a critic were the literature of the nineteenth and early twentieth centuries (especially American, Russian, English, and Italian) and literary theory (especially the theory of the novel and the relation of art to morality), but the full scope of his criticism includes much more: the "Study of Thomas Hardy," for instance, is, among other things, a wide-ranging interpretation of Western literature and art.

The undervaluation of Lawrence as a critic may be due in part to the long inaccessibility of essential sources, for *Phoenix* has only recently been reissued and the scattered letters only recently collected.[3] But I believe there are more basic causes, inherent in the criticism itself—namely, its peculiarities of form, of tone, and of style.

Lawrencean criticism proceeds quite deliberately beyond the bound which formal criticism usually sets for itself: the elucidation of text and the relation of text to literary tradition. A good deal of modern formal criticism is, we are beginning to realize, more ideological than it pretends to be, but seldom is it so directly harnessed to such an explicit and individual moral vision. In *Studies,* for instance, on which his reputation as a critic chiefly rests, Lawrence sets himself not only

2. This means that Lawrence's view of a particular writer or book must be pieced together from a variety of sources. There is, for instance, no essay by Lawrence on Tolstoi specifically, yet Tolstoi was one of the writers he was most interested in. To get Lawrence's full view of him we must turn to "Study of Thomas Hardy," *Fantasia of the Unconscious,* the preface to his translation of Verga's *Cavelleria Rusticana,* "The Novel" from *Reflections on the Death of a Porcupine, Apocalypse,* and several poems. For this reason, I have listed in an appendix the writers on whom Lawrence has made some significant comment, together with the places in his work where that comment may be found. The appendix should also help to give some idea of the range and focus of his literary interests.

3. *The Collected Letters of D. H. Lawrence,* ed. Harry Moore (2 vols. New York, 1962). This is a compilation from many sources (including the old, standard Huxley volume), some previously unpublished, but it is not complete.

a literary task, "to save the tale from the artist who created it" (*S* 13), but also a prophetic task, to be "midwife to the homunculus" of a new era (*S* 8); his only other critical work of book length which proposes a literary subject, the "Study of Thomas Hardy" (unless we include *Apocalypse,* which is in this respect similar), combines literary criticism with art criticism, social and political criticism, and metaphysics.

The flexible, freewheeling form of critical essay which Lawrence developed for himself enabled him to pass naturally beyond a concern for art proper and to emphasize its relation to the civilization of which it is a vital expression. He sometimes flouted distinctions between fiction and fact—linking, for example, Hamlet and Napoleon, *The Idiot* and President Wilson (*P* 541, 318), using both terms as symbols in a vast and tendentious historical myth—but it is essential to understand that he was keenly sensitive to aesthetic values. Art was for him both text and pretext, but its moral usefulness depended on its first being art. It was to art that he so often turned in his search for values, because he had made an assumption that was as fundamentally aesthetic as moral—namely, that "Art-speech is the only truth" (*S* 12). By this Lawrence meant, first, that genuine art represents the deepest penetration of the human consciousness into reality, and, second, that "if it be really a work of art it must contain the essential criticism on the morality to which it adheres" (*P* 476) and is therefore truer than any discursive statement. Similarly, the distinction between art and artist, which he also sometimes flouted superficially, was in fact essential to his critical objective, which was "to save the tale from the artist who created it," to reveal deeper and truer implications of a work than the artist himself may have been conscious of. It must be added that in the process of this revelation the critic tried, often successfully, to identify the truth in the work with the truth of his own moral vision, to merge what the work *really* says with what it should say.

To conduct criticism of this kind, Lawrence required a standard of value. He most often called this standard "life" and identified it both with "true emotion" within the individual soul and "true relationship" between self and otherness. Both true emotion and true relationship are norms, but flexible rather than fixed. They may change within the wide limits of vital possibility, limits that are to be defined only by

3

the points beyond which the soul and relationship lose their natural subtlety and fluidity. Such a collapse may be caused by the erection of some fixed and permanent standard, the idealization of one direction of consciousness. Lawrence scolded Plato and Jesus, for instance, for making one emotion supreme; balance could not so easily be restored, because idealization tended thereafter to predetermine the naturally indeterminate vital consciousness. A paradox essential to Lawrence's thought, then, and one by which he escapes total relativism as well as total absolutism, is that life is both incorruptible (thereby absolute) and vulnerable (thereby subject to perversion by the force in man and, ultimately, in civilization that seeks fixity, finality, and changelessness.)[4]

This belief underlies his approach to art. On the one hand, no art can be wholly false because art *qua* art in some degree honors life—"in their passional inspiration, [artists] are all phallic worshippers" (*R* 105–06) was one way Lawrence liked to express it—and to that degree partakes of absolute value. But, on the other hand, no art can be wholly true, because the artist's emphasis will be inescapably relative to his time and place; for the artist of the modern epoch especially, the influence of civilization is likely to be reflected in art not only as metaphysical imbalance but also as a fear of the unknown, of openness to possibility, which inhibits or perverts the artist's very capacity to honor life.

4. For the words incorruptible and vulnerable in this context I am indebted to Leone Vivante's *A Philosophy of Potentiality* (London, 1955):

> Subjective or living being is represented in Lawrence as an immense cosmic positivity, not rigid, not mechanical. It shares in the nature of intrinsic purposiveness. It is something really positive, not inertial. It is obscure, almost formless, but not absolutely formless, not absolutely timeless; not extra-phenomenal. It is urgent, relentless. Yet delicate, soft, tender. Somehow vulnerable, essentially so, and yet incorruptible. . . . An infinite urge for form and materialization. Ever potential, never defined.   [p. 101]

There is a striking similarity between this description and M. H. Abrams' description of the Romantic metaphor of the correspondent breeze, which is delicate and gentle but fierce and destructive, a symbol of the creative imagination. See "The Correspondent Breeze: A Romantic Metaphor," in *English Romantic Poets: Modern Essays in Criticism,* ed. M. H. Abrams (New York, 1960), pp. 37–54. Indeed, Lawrence uses the metaphor with the same significance: e.g. *CP* 250 and *SM* 30.

It was primarily the "errors" of art and artist that concerned Lawrence: their deviation from the norm of "life," sometimes conceived as the hidden numen behind phenomena, sometimes as the gamut of vital possibility, and even as the one thing needful for our time. He was too engaged a writer, too intent upon changing the world he lived in, to observe the oscillations and perversions of vital consciousness from a lofty metaphysical perch. At the risk of being misunderstood or subject to correction himself at the next turn of history, he wanted to find and declare "the truth that concerns us, whether it concerns our grandchildren or not" (*S* 12). He read literature mainly as a diagnosis of our psychic illness. The necessary truth of art he sometimes took for granted, particularly in his less deliberate remarks; the falsehood provoked him to rage.

This peculiarity of tone may lead one to suppose, quite mistakenly, that Lawrence's criticism is merely negative and reductive. When he suppresses the positive value that is necessarily implied in his view of art, it is important to remember that the judgment is, so far as art and artist are concerned, partial. I do not wish to suggest that Lawrence's criticism is balanced and reasonable, for it is not, but only that it is more complex and less reductive than may be supposed.

In a sense, "reductive" is a particularly inappropriate description of Lawrence's criticism, despite its partisanship, for the critic's rage, oddly, enhances rather than diminishes the work being discussed. W. H. Auden perceived this when he wrote of Lawrence, "He is so passionately interested in the work he is talking about and so little interested in his reputation as a critic that, even when he is violently and quite unfairly attacking an author, he makes him sound far more exciting and worth reading than most critics make one sound whom they are professing to praise."[5] Although I should think one would have to find the critic's assumptions interesting and provisionally valid, it is not their final truth that need concern us; rather, we want to know how good a criticism they make for. And the point to be made here is that Lawrence's partisanship does not in itself vitiate that criticism. The Baudelairean prescription which Martin Turnell uses as an epigraph in "An Essay on Criticism" applies perfectly, as Turnell intends it should, to Lawrence: "Criticism should be partial, passionate,

5. "Some Notes on D. H. Lawrence," *The Nation* (April 26, 1947), p. 482.

and political, that is to say, it must be written from an exclusive point of view, but from a point of view which opens up the widest horizons."[6] One of the most wholesome influences of Lawrence as a critic is that, for all his improprieties, he takes literature more seriously than do many of us; unhesitatingly, he sees it as intensely relevant to the human situation. It is this passionate and encompassing sense of life that explains why even his terse and angry squibs are often richly suggestive.

Lawrence's moral earnestness is rather different from that of most other critics. They assess the merit of an artist's intention along with the skill of his execution. Lawrence usually takes these for granted, saying little about artists he does not think important, for "only the best matters" (*CP* 668). He gauges instead their courage and sincerity, the human qualities he most admires and so markedly possesses: Courage is "the only thing worth having anyhow" (*CB* 3 8); "Before everything I like sincerity, and a quickening spontaneous emotion" (*CL* 21). Implied in this attitude is a profound faith in what men could be at their best and a profound resistance to what they settle for from timidity and ignorance. Thus he criticizes a book on the basis of what it should mean, identified if possible with what it does mean when read in depth. He berates an author not so much for failing as an artist as for failing as a man to realize the full implications of his work. As Richard Rees put it, "Lawrence could hate, but I believe he was incapable of feeling contempt."[7]

Lawrence's manner of confronting fellow artists has not been well understood. He was in a significant sense the least arrogant of critics. It was in fact because the usual critical stance seemed to him an affectation of superiority, an impertinence, that he dismounted and took up hand-to-hand combat.[8] He scolded, ridiculed, and first-

6. Martin Turnell, "An Essay on Criticism," *Dublin Review,* 444 (1948), p. 89.

7. *Brave Men: A Study of D. H. Lawrence and Simone Weil* (Carbondale, Ill., 1959), p. 18.

8. To Amy Lowell he wrote: "If the critics are not less than the authors they criticize, they will at once burst into equal authorship. And being less than the authors they criticize, they must diminish these authors. For no critic can admit anything bigger than himself" (*SL* 82–83). In a review: "I have tried more or less to give a *résumé* of Dr. Burrow's book. I feel there is a certain impertinence in giving these *résumés*. But not more than in the

named his subjects, but not to reduce a reputation or indulge his angry wit.[9] It was always the issue that engaged him. One critic describes the encounter as "a dynamic conflict of value systems in which Lawrence always seems to win, if only . . . because he rarely tackles any writer whose position he does not think he can improve upon."[1] But Lawrence "improves" on writers not to win a personal combat but to declare, on behalf of all men subjected to the same ideological pressures, a certain vision of life. Graham Hough puts it more carefully: "He exposes the weaknesses of civilization, rather than of individual authors. He blames it, not them, that we are not phallic worshippers."[2] Indeed, for Lawrence all genuine artists are culture *heroes*. And that fact should help us emend Leslie Fiedler's petulant criticism: "Only D. H. Lawrence has ever challenged Whitman's claim to this honor [celebrator of the body]. . . . But one can hardly expect Lawrence to be fair since he coveted for himself the title of the anti-Christian Christ."[3] "Fair" he may not be (although, since according to the Lawrencean psychology the celebration of the body may derive either from blood *or* mental consciousness, the challenge to Whitman is not on the face of it merely perverse or spiteful), but the role in which he casts Whitman finally ("the one man breaking a way ahead"—*S* 183) is hardly a secondary one.

It is partly true of course, as Fiedler implies, that Lawrence tends to make his heroes forerunners to his own gospel. But that contributes to the excitement of his criticism. It is synthetic as well as analytic. Watching Lawrence struggle with himself while he struggles

----

affectation of 'criticizing' and being superior" (*P* 382). In another: "It would be easy enough to rise in critical superiority as a critic always feels he must and find fault" (*P* 336). In short, Lawrence scorned carping and disparaging: his quarrel went deeper.

 9. Lawrence's wit is uninhibited but essentially serious, unlike Pound's, which is often merely flippant and naughty. Pound's slanginess is partly avant-garde affectation, from which Lawrence (who is even fastidiously conservative in some respects, such as spelling) is quite free.

 1. Ralph Maud, "D. H. Lawrence: True Emotion as Ethical Control in Art," *Western Humanities Review*, 9 (1955), p. 233.

 2. Graham Hough, *The Dark Sun: A Study of D. H. Lawrence* (New York, 1957), p. 237.

 3. Leslie Fiedler, *An End to Innocence* (Boston, 1955), pp. 159–60.

with his subject, one senses a developing artistic structure, a myth in the process of being forged.

No doubt this raises a troublesome problem. At what point does the subject become irrelevant; at what point could the critic as well be discussing anything at all; or, to put it another way, at what point does either the subject or the critic's world view come to seem an intrusion? Martin Turnell, who values personal force above all else in the critic and who therefore has a very high opinion of Lawrence's criticism, feels that the critic is an artist expressing himself through other artists. "He must not distort their vision, but he must communicate *himself* to the reader."[4] That Lawrence succeeds in the latter will not be doubted. The extent to which he distorts the vision of others is a problem that will be considered in the course of this study.

A tone of anger, in any case, is no reliable indication of Lawrence's estimate of particular authors or works. His anger may properly attach to the historical tendency reflected in the work; a work may even be denounced for its ideological one-sidedness, yet approved precisely for revealing that danger to us. Moreover, the critic may be most severe where he admires most (as with *Anna Karenina*), on the principle that great work is worth quarreling with while lesser work is not: as he once wrote of a minor Hardy novel, "The spirit being small, the complaint is narrow" (*P* 435). Readers who are confused by such integration of censure and praise are, I suspect, adhering to the notion that criticism should give grades rather than explore the sometimes contrary implications of a work of art; the dialectical critic seems to them merely illogical. Confronted with Lawrence's vituperations, we should remember that he maintained the profoundest respect for literature, following his own precept: "To my thinking, the critic, like a good beadle, should rap the public on the knuckles and make it attend during divine service. And any good book is a divine service" (*P* 237).

Lawrence's gift for animated and—despite repetitiveness—incisive discourse is obvious, yet, strangely, he does put a considerable burden on the reader who would follow his argument closely. I believe this is due to an essential peculiarity of his style, a peculiarity reflected in violations of logic and in shifting, inconsistent, and symbolic termi-

4. Turnell, *Dublin Review*, 444, 94–95.

nology. It is not, I think, sufficiently acknowledged or understood by his critics: F. R. Leavis hardly seems aware of it, Graham Hough considers it superficial, and T. S. Eliot describes it as Lawrence's "incapacity for what we ordinarily call thinking."[5] Aldous Huxley, addressing himself to Eliot's charge, points out that Lawrence did not reject what we ordinarily call thinking because of incapacity but because "the methods of science and critical philosophy were incompatible with the exercise of his gift—the immediate perception and artistic rendering of divine otherness" (*L* xv). Huxley presents Lawrence as a man who, even in critical discourse, must be an artist. There is in fact a certain subjective immediacy in his criticism as in his art, an attempt to render "the felt quality of experience,"[6] although we should understand that Lawrence's critical intelligence is manifest the way any good critical intelligence is manifest: in the penetration of the questions asked, in the subtlety and flexibility with which discriminations are made, and in the skill with which arguments are sustained.

Lawrence's subjectivity must be distinguished from what might be called "subjectivism," implying a personal or egoistic bias and permitting a fixed, consistent point of view. Subjectivity, or "true knowing," being rooted in the blood rather than the mind, is to be regarded as flexible rather than fixed, as impersonal rather than personal, and even, when opposed to subjectivism (an expression of the detested mental consciousness), as objective. Lawrence sometimes identifies it with the unconscious, but prefers to think of it positively as simply another kind of consciousness: hence his use of such terms as blood consciousness, physical consciousness, and phallic consciousness.

The effort to present the felt quality of thought leads naturally to metaphor, and Lawrence often employs metaphors as conceptual categories in his criticism. But, having turned to them for their greater emotional precision, he seems to resent their logical imprecision and to insist, in both art and criticism, that he is *not* using

5. See F. R. Leavis, *D. H. Lawrence: Novelist* (London, 1955), pp. 303–11, and the reviews in *Scrutiny* of *The Letters of D. H. Lawrence* (1932–33), of *After Strange Gods* (1934–35), and of *Phoenix* (1937–38); Hough, *The Dark Sun*, p. 218; and T. S. Eliot, *After Strange Gods* (New York, 1933), p. 63.
6. I take the phrase from Eliseo Vivas, *D. H. Lawrence: The Failure and the Triumph of Art* (Evanston, Ill., 1960), p. 204.

metaphor but expressing the literal truth. Mrs. Ruskin need not have said that her husband should have married his mother: "he *was* married to his mother" (*F* 153–54). For Lawrence inner vision seemed truer than outer vision, and he resisted a mere equation of the two. Like his own Count Dionys in "The Ladybird," he seemed to look at life inside out, presenting noumenal events with the literalness we expect in a description of phenomenal events.

One could say, employing a distinction made by Charles Feidelson, that Lawrence resisted the structure of symbolism, which presents opposed elements in a unity, and preferred the structure of dialectic, which asserts the unity as a logical proposition.[7] Skeptical of the result, he constantly shifted the term that was to serve him as a standard. Among his many normative terms were blood, sensual, passional, phallic, and human consciousness; intuitive, spontaneous, and naïve self; the quick, the soul, the Holy Ghost, and Life. One of his favorites was "Holy Ghost," which recommended itself because of its very elusiveness ("you can't lay salt on its tail"—*P* 652), and its progress in Lawrence's criticism is instructive. It reigns supreme in *Studies* of 1923. By 1925 its elevation has become precarious: "Only the Holy Ghost knows what righteousness is. And heaven only knows what the Holy Ghost is! But it sounds all right" (*R* 121). A few years later it has fallen:[8] "It is difficult to know what name to give to that most central and vital clue to the human being, which clinches him into integrity. The best is to call it his vital sanity. We thus escape the rather nauseating emotional suggestions of words like soul and spirit and holy ghost" (*P* 766). Trying to write about the deep life of the spirit in a language used for other purposes and in an age in which mass communication rapidly caused fresh phraseology to become stale, Lawrence was struggling with language itself. His very aggressiveness hints at the magnitude of his effort.

Unlike Blake, however, he did not devise a private vocabulary, nor did he regularly avoid the given terms of conceptual discourse. Thus many terms which he does use throughout his work—e.g. conscious-

7. Charles Feidelson, *Symbolism and American Literature* (Chicago, 1953), p. 70.

8. This passage is from an essay ("Introduction to Pictures," in *Phoenix*) which cannot be definitively dated but which on internal evidence may safely be supposed to have been written between 1927 and 1929.

ness, knowing, imagination, spirit, objectivity, subjectivity, and even mind—can be honorific or pejorative, depending on whether they are understood as referring to the true consciousness or the false. At times, such indicative adjectives as pure, real, true, or their opposites may precede these nouns, but often not.

What makes the problem more acute than it need be is that Lawrence sometimes expresses whatever part of the truth he happens to be discussing with such positiveness and finality that he implies an absolute truth where he intends a relative one. In short, he overstates, and he must retract a little if he would make his meaning clear. Whitman is at first simply a "post-mortem" poet, but some pages later a poet whose doctrine brought him "to the Edge of Death" (*S* 174, 191); "Turner is a lie, and Raphael is a lie," but a few paragraphs later, "almost a lie, almost a blasphemy" (*P* 475–76). The qualification is characteristically made reluctantly or parenthetically, and sometimes not at all. But it is necessarily implied whenever Lawrence categorically denounces any genuine art or, for that matter, any genuine passion of the human soul, which cannot in his view be utterly false or misguided.

Lawrence's criticism is not logically consistent,[9] not even as consistent as it might be on its own premises, but if we understand its peculiarities, we will discover that it is fundamentally coherent.

Given the kind of writer Lawrence is—so much of a piece and yet so easily misleading in isolated remarks—it is clear that his

9. A less drastic but still significant kind of inconsistency follows from his very mode of composition, his well-known distaste for close revision in favor of "saying the whole thing again." This results in a certain amount of groping and shifting of ground, expressed stylistically in two principal ways: first, in the frequency of negative conjunctions, giving the impression of extemporaneous thinking (e.g. "This is the trouble with Verga. But on the other hand, everything he does has a weird quality of Verga in it, quite distinct and like nothing else. And yet, perhaps the gross vision of the man is not quite his own. All his movements are his own. But his main motive is borrowed"— *P* 225); second, in incremental discriminations (e.g. he speaks at one point of the twofold utterance of religious art and tragic art, and, a moment later, having worked out his thought further, he makes this a threefold utterance: religion, religious art, and tragic art—*P* 449–50).

literary criticism cannot satisfactorily be segregated from his work as a whole. In discussing earlier the possible misunderstanding of Lawrence's tone, I would have spoken of the danger of considering his critical opinions out of context, except that the proper context is often not simply the particular work in which the opinion is found but the various works in which the author or work in question is treated or in which aspects of the critical method or doctrine are clarified. I observed at the outset that literary criticism is a major *area* of Lawrence's achievement, but it would be more accurate to call it a major *expression* of his achievement, as his art is another expression of the same whole.

The studies that have thus far been made of Lawrence's criticism specifically are few and limited in scope,[1] nor has any of the other studies of his art or thought dealt with it extensively. But because an understanding of the criticism depends very much on an understanding of Lawrence generally, I have been aided by a number of essays which do not demarcate the literary criticism specifically as a subject of study.[2] For the same reason, what I take to be a proper view of the criticism is still much obstructed by the opposed formulations of T. S. Eliot and F. R. Leavis, and I would like briefly to discuss this difference in order to clarify the view of Lawrence which I shall take.

---

1. Aside from various reviews of posthumously issued compilations of Lawrence's criticism and aside from incidental praise, particularly of *Studies,* by various influential critics such as Edmund Wilson, W. H. Auden, Lionel Trilling, Alfred Kazin, Martin Turnell, and Leslie Fiedler, these include the following: William Deakin, "Lawrence's Attack on Joyce and Proust," *Essays in Criticism* (October 1957), pp. 383–403; Ralph Maud, "True Emotion as Ethical Control in Art," *Western Humanities Review, 9,* pp. 230–40; and, the only one of significance, Richard Foster, "Criticism as Rage," in *A D. H. Lawrence Miscellany,* H. T. Moore, ed. (Carbondale, Ill., 1959). In addition, Armin Arnold, in *D. H. Lawrence and America* (New York, 1959) and again in *The Symbolic Meaning,* has made a close but pedestrian collation of the versions of *Studies.*

2. I have profited particularly from reading Alfred Kazin, Richard Foster, and Martin Turnell on moral force in literary criticism; Leone Vivante and Joyce Cary on some premises of Lawrence's aesthetic theory; Kingsley Widmer and Norman Mailer on the nature of the demonic; and Northrop Frye and Harold Bloom on mythopoeia and Lawrence's affinity to the Romantic tradition.

Introduction

In *After Strange Gods* Eliot wrote:

> I have already touched upon the deplorable religious upbring-
> ing which gave Lawrence his lust for intellectual independence:
> like most people who do not know what orthodoxy is he hated
> it. And I have already mentioned the insensibility to ordinary
> social morality, which is so alien to my mind that I am com-
> pletely baffled by it as a monstrosity. The point is that Lawrence
> started life wholly free from any restriction of tradition or
> institution, that he had no guidance except the Inner Light,
> the most untrustworthy and deceitful guide that ever offered
> itself to wandering humanity. It was peculiarly so of Lawrence,
> who does not seem to have been gifted with the faculty of
> self-criticism, except in flashes, even to the extent of ordinary
> worldly shrewdness. Of divine illumination, it may be said
> that any man is likely to think that he has it when he has it
> not; and even when he has it, the daily man that he is may
> draw the wrong conclusions from the enlightenment which
> the momentary man has received: no one, in short, can be the
> sole judge of whence his inspiration comes. A man like Law-
> rence, therefore, with his acute sensibility, violent prejudices
> and passions, and lack of intellectual and social training, is
> admirably fitted to be an instrument for the forces of good or
> for the forces of evil.[3]

Eliot, one feels—apart simply from the prejudices of his position—
was not patient enough to understand Lawrence fully, to understand
chiefly that essential self-criticism which is so thoroughly implicit
in both his criticism and his art. Had he been so, he might have
granted Lawrence the respect he grants to Blake, for his approach
is about the same in both cases, and we would have at least the Eliot
who, in Alfred Kazin's words, "managed to say exactly the right
things about Blake's imaginative independence, and to draw the
wrong conclusions."[4] Yet with his keen eye for heresy, Eliot has
perceived more truly than many sympathetic critics the basic radical-
ism of Lawrence's thought, and has put the issue squarely in con-
trasting independence and the Inner Light to tradition and institution.
    Almost everything Eliot has written of Lawrence has been rebutted

3. *After Strange Gods,* pp. 63–64.
4. "The Function of Criticism Today," *Commentary* (November 1960),
p. 374.

point by point by Leavis. I am reluctant to quarrel with a man who has long maintained a high regard for Lawrence's criticism (and who can be very keen when he stops polemicizing), but Leavis, instead of questioning the very prejudice against individual authority, has tacitly accepted it, and with what Kingsley Widmer neatly termed "a moralistic righteousness which is simply an inversion of Eliot's,"[5] has tried to show that Lawrence is really a saner, sounder, fairer critic than anyone else in his day. Leavis speaks, for example, of Lawrence's "unfailing sense of difference between what makes for life and what doesn't, between what tends toward health, and what away from health."[6] Very well, but it is not clear that what Leavis means by life is what Lawrence means by it. Does Leavis understand, for instance, that the path to Lawrencean life leads very often through death?

The distortion risked by this approach is perhaps more evident in the work of lesser critics, for Leavis' own rage preserves something of the Lawrencean spirit. G. S. Fraser notes "that the central standard by which Lawrence seems to judge [literature] is a classical one: 'Nothing too much.'"[7] And Ralph Maud, also finding Lawrence a critic who shies from extremes, feels that he would have won the approval of Irving Babbitt![8] In this case as in others, a radical thinker seems to be better understood by his conservative counterpart than by his liberal sympathizers.

Lawrence did indeed attack one-sidedness, but not because he sought to refurbish the classical ideal of balance based on the concept of the mean and on the assumption of an order or authority external to the individual. He sought instead the Romantic ideal of a new center of consciousness which would transcend (or subtend) the dualism of mind and body and which would be the basis of a new idea of community. The balance that Lawrence wanted would permit all desires their full natural expression—i.e. their expression up to the point beyond which they ceased to be spontaneous and became

5. Kingsley Widmer, "Our Demonic Heritage," in Moore, *A D. H. Lawrence Miscellany*, p. 25 n.
6. F. R. Leavis, "Mr. Eliot and Lawrence," in *The Achievement of D. H. Lawrence,* ed. with intro. by F. J. Hoffman and H. T. Moore (Norman, Okla., 1953), p. 104.
7. G. S. Fraser, *The Modern Writer and His World* (London, 1953), p. 309.
8. Maud, *Western Humanities Review, 9,* 233.

mechanical, ceased to be actions and became reactions, ceased to derive from the unknown well of the creative unconscious and became repetitions of already known actions and utterances. Particularly in the modern age, the ideological climate of which, so Lawrence felt, was clogged with dead ideals, and particularly for the artist, whose business it was as the "growing tip" of the "living, extending consciousness" to find a new vital utterance, this meant turning not toward the mean but toward the extreme; it meant getting beyond the known (often with some destructive violence, since the dead ideals were so oppressive) to the unknown. But the extreme must not become another fixed idea, another idealism. Hence the principle stated in "Education of the People" and basic to his thinking: "One should go to the extremity of any experience. But that one should stay there, and make a habit of the extreme, is another matter" (P 653). This required courage and discipline, courage to go to the extreme and discipline to maintain, in doing so, the integrity of one's vital being. Discipline is not a word we associate with Lawrence, but a principle of restraint is in fact necessary to any voluntarist position that does not ask us simply to embrace chaos. For Lawrence there *are* limits, but man too quickly decides what they are. And the institutionalization of any limit or form, no matter how generously conceived, causes it to degenerate into a mechanical principle.

In application this theory remains subtle and complex. In *Studies,* for example, Lawrence both berates and admires the Americans for their extremity of vision, verging on death. He does so because he perceives in their art the simultaneous activity of two modes of consciousness: the ego or mental consciousness and the living or blood consciousness. In the mind death is a fixed idea and hampers development. In the blood it is part of life, a step to something beyond, for in true life-development there is no end, no final word. Lawrence once remarked that the greatest men for him were Dante, Leonardo, Beethoven, and Whitman. The remark is interesting because it can hardly be explained by ideological congruity and because, Whitman excepted, these are not men whom he otherwise extols. I suspect that he linked them because he believed that they had achieved an extreme vision *without ceasing to be artists,* without forsaking the inherent subtlety of art-speech.

Lawrence's world view, then, is not simply a version or inversion of classical humanism or Judeo-Christianity, although comparisons to these are sometimes in order. It resembles perhaps more closely the cosmology of the early Greek philosophers, although its orientation is far more anthropocentric, and ancient Eastern thought, although it is far more empirical, activist, and utopian. For all his hearkening back to the wisdom of earlier ages, Lawrence's world view is essentially modern and, I think, essentially Romantic. He tried to synthesize the naturalism of a scientific age and the supernaturalism of a religious age. He both adhered to the immediate and actual and aspired to the ultimate and transcendent. One can only sum up his position in some paradoxical phrase such as Aldous Huxley's "mystical materialism" or Northrop Frye's "apocalyptic humanism." But probably too much has already been written about Lawrence's ideas in themselves, and I shall not expatiate upon them except to clarify some specifically literary problem.

·⊢————————————⊣·

The difficulty of segregating Lawrence's literary criticism from his general criticism, or even from his art, indicates the usefulness of a comprehensive study and, at the same time, the problems involved in organizing such a study. An arrangement by authors or groups of authors with whom he deals, by genres or periods, or by his own chronological development would be artificial and would not take us to the center of the subject. These schemes will be used now and then, but it seems best to proceed in the main by a different principle, to view the whole subject from a different perspective in each chapter, even at the risk of some overlapping.

Basically then, this is a study of Lawrence from the vantage of his literary criticism. The central focus is the critic's moral argument: its relation to aesthetic judgment and theory, its sensitivity to unconscious meanings, and its pervasive prophetic intention. The unifying theme, loosely woven throughout, may be described as Lawrence in the Romantic tradition.

2

The Critic

Although Lawrence wrote little about literary criticism and the literary critic as such, the page-and-a-half introduction to his study of John Galsworthy states his fundamental position and may usefully be taken as a point of departure. It begins:

> Literary criticism can be no more than a reasoned account of the feeling produced upon the critic by the book he is criticizing. Criticism can never be a science: it is, in the first place, much too personal, and in the second, it is concerned with values that science ignores. The touchstone is emotion, not reason. We judge a work of art by its effect on our sincere and vital emotion, and nothing else. All the critical twiddle-twaddle about style and form, all this pseudo-scientific classifying and analyzing of books in an imitation-botanical fashion, is mere impertinence and mostly dull jargon. [P 539]

We should not understand this too quickly. It is clearly a rejection of Outside Authority and may therefore suggest Whiggery to T. S. Eliot, but Lawrence is not endorsing the doctrine of doing as one likes. "It is never freedom till you find something you *positively want to be*" (S 14, Lawrence's italics). "Liberty is a changing of prisons, to those who seek only liberty."[1] If then he is advocating

1. D. H. Lawrence and M. L. Skinner, *The Boy in the Bush* (London, 1924), p. 33. One hesitates to quote from this novel since it is a collaboration or,

an impressionistic criticism, we may suppose that it is of a more disciplined and rigorous kind than might be inferred from this paragraph.

The "touchstone is emotion, not reason." In what sense is he using these words? We note that the key term "emotion" is subjected to the controlling adjectives "vital" and "sincere," which are in turn implicitly defined in the succeeding paragraphs:

> A critic must be able to *feel* the impact of a work of art in all its complexity and force. To do so, he must be a man of force and complexity himself, which few critics are. A man with a paltry, impudent nature will never write anything but paltry, impudent criticism. And a man who is emotionally educated is as rare as a phoenix. The more scholastically educated a man is generally, the more he is an emotional boor.
>
> More than this, even an artistically and emotionally educated man must be a man of good faith. He must have the courage to *admit* what he feels, as well as the flexibility to *know* what he feels. So Sainte-Beuve remains to me, a great critic. And a man like Macaulay, brilliant as he is, is unsatisfactory because he is not honest. He is emotionally very alive, but he juggles his feelings. He prefers a fine effect to the sincere statement of the aesthetic and emotional reaction. He is quite intellectually capable of giving us a true account of what he feels. But not morally. A critic must be emotionally alive in every fibre, intellectually capable and skilful in essential logic, and then morally very honest.
>
> Then it seems to me a good critic should give his readers a few standards to go by. He can change his standards for every new critical attempt, so long as he keeps good faith. But it is just as well to say: This and this is the standard we judge by. [*P* 539]

"Vital" is rephrased as "the flexibility to *know* what he feels" and "emotionally alive in every fibre"; "sincere" becomes "the courage to *admit* what he feels" and "morally very honest." The sharp distinction

---

more exactly, a thorough rewriting by Lawrence of Mollie Skinner's manuscript. But this passage, like many others, has an unquestionably Lawrencean ring. That "the deep instincts are moral" (*CP* 529) is a central idea in Lawrence's thought. In another phrasing of it: "The only rule is, do what you *really*, impulsively, wish to do. But always act on your own responsibility, sincerely. And have the courage of your own strong emotion" (*F* 89).

between emotion and reason is thus modified, for knowing and admitting imply some degree of intellection. Apparently Lawrence is thinking of emotion as possessing a cognitive capacity. The good critic is emotionally educated, has complexity as well as force. And note the assimilation of "artistically" and "aesthetic" to "emotionally" and "emotion": "More than this, even an artistically and emotionally educated man"; "the sincere statement of the aesthetic and emotional reaction." That Lawrence understood criticism to require what we usually call intelligence is also indicated by his insertion of the third term, "intellectually capable and skilful in essential logic," in his summary of requisites for the critic. But again the addition is made rather surreptitiously. It is as if he wants to avoid any word or phrase which too clearly suggests mental consciousness: the word "essential" is apparently present to protect this added requisite from such an implication.[2]

The choice of the word "reason" as the antithesis of "emotion" becomes part of the strategy. Lawrence can more easily establish a cognitive meaning for emotion by adopting the antithetical term least likely to suggest thought in its subjective aspect, and he associates reason with science to reinforce its restricted meaning.

But if Lawrence did not in fact intend so sharp a cleavage between feeling and thought, we may wonder why he states the matter in this way. It is not mere impatience that causes him to use language "straightforwardly to the point of sloppiness," in R. P. Blackmur's phrase.[3] Partly it is his deep resistance to the kind of discipline that checks the flow of impassioned thought—a discipline he would have called self-consciousness, as opposed to self-awareness (the distinction will concern us in the following chapter)—and partly it is simply his practical difficulty in finding some middle term, a difficulty that arises because, in his view, words denoting thought or judgment

2. A similar procedure is followed in his essay "The Novel" (*R* 103–23). Lawrence cites three requisites for the novel: it must be quick; interrelated in all its parts, vitally, organically; and honorable—which incidentally bear a striking resemblance to the three requisites for the critic—and again to the second item of the list are added protective modifiers, apparently so that "interrelated" should not suggest too intellectual or formal a criterion.

3. R. P. Blackmur, "D. H. Lawrence and Expressive Form," in his *Form and Value in Modern Poetry* (New York, 1957), p. 260.

become ambiguous—that is, they can refer to the mental consciousness or to the emotional consciousness, and Lawrence clearly wanted
to establish the seat of true judgment in the latter. He did not scorn
intellect itself, but he often found it necessary to scorn the word
(and its relatives). Nor, for several reasons, could he use "imagination,"
that good word of Romantic criticism, as a workable middle term:
it was too closely associated with sight, with outer rather than inner
vision—a consideration that also somewhat deterred Wordsworth,
who shared Lawrence's feeling about the despotism of the eye; it
suggested self-consciousness and thus an obstruction to contact with
otherness; and it looked before and after, drawing us away from the
intense immediacy of the present.[4]

Yet Lawrence was not one to assume a defensive posture, and so
we find in his work the familiar terms of intellection employed in a
positive sense, wrested, as it were, from the mental consciousness.
This is especially true of words such as "knowing" and "thought,"
which suggest depth in consciousness. Thus, "I know nothing about
it. I only know you aren't right" (*L* 155). Or, "Thought, I love
thought. / But not the jaggling and twisting of already existent ideas"
(*CP* 673). And, in fact, so energetic was Lawrence's effort to subdue
the vocabulary of intellection to what for him was the primary
consciousness that he is not quite content to let even "Reason" get
away: "if we pause to think about it, we shall realize that it is not
Reason herself whom we have to defy, it is her myrmidons, our accepted ideas and thought forms" (*P* 297). There is "the pure mind, the
true reason, which is surely noble," degraded by Dostoevsky (*L* 313).
We can even turn again to the opening sentence of the very passage
in which we have examined his pitting of emotion against reason:
"Literary criticism can be no more than a *reasoned* account of the
feelings produced upon the critic by the book he is criticizing."[5]

4. Only in three places ("Introduction to These Paintings," a review of
Frederick Carter's *Dragon of the Apocalypse,* and *Apocalypse*) does he freely
use the word imagination in a positive sense. And in each he makes a point
of explaining that it is a faculty involving the whole of man's nature.
5. Lawrence actually read fairly extensively the reasoned accounts of scholars, particularly in the fields of history and anthropology, although he insisted
even there on the superiority of intuitive to rational knowledge. He considered
them useful either as stimulants of intuition (he asks for a *thin* book on Egypt,
because "The disputations of scholars are so boring and I like to fill in the

Emotion, then—but vital, sincere emotion—is to be the critic's source of judgment. If it seems to us that the value of a criticism practiced according to this theory is largely dependent on the skill of the practitioner, that the theory gains in weight when the critic's name is D. H. Lawrence, I think he himself has implied as much: "A critic must be able to *feel* the impact of a work in all its complexity and force. To do this, he must be a man of force and complexity himself, which few critics are." Such a conclusion modifies the absoluteness attributed to individual judgment, but Lawrence would not settle for a lesser truth than he himself could envision nor for a lesser force than he himself possessed.

This trust in emotion helps to explain, or perhaps is simply a way of describing, the most obvious quality of Lawrence's literary criticism: its extraordinary independence.[6] In substance, method, and style it

---

subject for myself"—*L* 318) or as supplements to it (considering the historical accuracy of A. F. Grazzini's Renaissance novella, *The Story of Doctor Manente,* he writes: "It sounds so true, it must be true. Meanwhile someone ought to annotate [Grazzini] and verify his allusions where possible"—*P* 278).

6. His independence of mind was evident remarkably early, although he had to struggle for maturity of expression. His youthful (i.e. pre-1910) reactions to literature, as recorded mainly by the Chambers sisters, interestingly reveal an already distinctive sensibility and a not yet distinctive voice. May Chambers remembered that he preferred David Copperfield's Dora to Agnes, "because she was gay, even useless, rather than serious" (*CB* 3, 581). Jessie recalled that he could not forgive George Eliot for the proposed marriage of the vital Maggie Tulliver to the cripple Philip ("It's wrong, wrong. She should never make her do it.") and that he thought *Crime and Punishment* was "very great but I don't like it. I don't quite understand it" (*D. H. Lawrence: A Personal Record* [London, 1935], pp. 97, 123). The headmaster of the school where Lawrence taught from 1908 to 1911 adds an interesting note:

> Lawrence's choice of verse for class study was, for the time, unorthodox. He would have none of the "We Are Seven" etc. category. Nor would he tolerate any with what he called "a sniff of moral imposition." I found entered in his records such selections as "The Assyrian Came Down" (Byron), "The Bells of Shandon" (Mahoney), "Go Fetch Me a Pint of Wine" (Burns). He considered that the best approach to poetry for young people was through rhythm and the ring of words rather than the evasive appeal of an unreal and abstract morality.

This is quoted in Harry T. Moore, *The Intelligent Heart* (New York, 1954), p. 8.

Chapter Two

appears to be almost totally underived. But this has little or nothing
to do with his presumptive lack of "intellectual and social training."
Rather, Lawrence felt from deep conviction that anything derived or
borrowed would hinder him from recording his true reaction. Un-
doubtedly the correlation he proposes between scholastic education
and emotional boorishness is an oversimplification, but it is a sincere,
not merely spiteful, statement, and it helps to account for his consistent indifference to academic classifications and categories. He may
have conceded that an established methodology assists men of lesser
force and complexity to write at least competently about literature,
but this would not have recommended it to Lawrence himself.

Thoroughly independent as he is, Lawrence yet manages to escape
the perils of impressionistic subjectivism, because he judges by and
gives meaning to standards of his own devising. When he suggests,
in the passage quoted above, that a good critic should give his readers
a few standards to go by, he is only codifying his own practice, which
regularly establishes standards for each serious critical venture—e.g.
the human being versus the social being in "John Galsworthy,"
phallic consciousness versus ego consciousness in "The Novel," and
so forth. Yet he knows how to handle them flexibly. He erects a particular standard for a particular purpose, another for another purpose;
the chosen standard is not of course inconsistent with the absolute
value of "life" but is the one best suited by its nuances to test the
work at hand.

Lawrence's confrontation of other artists is assuredly personal:

> When a young painter studies an old master, he studies, not
> the form, that is an abstraction which does not exist: he studies
> maybe the method of the old great artist: but he studies chiefly
> to understand how the old great artist suffered in himself
> the conflict of Love and Law, and brought them to a reconcilia-

---

It is probably futile to speculate very far on the origins of Lawrence's
unusual independence since the final explanation must be inexplicable personal
genius. Some critics have emphasized the importance of his nonconformist
religious education. Some have noted as a contributing influence the provincial
background (in this connection see an interesting early letter by Lawrence in
CB 3, 608). And perhaps too his abnormally close relationship with his
mother was a source of strength as well as pain—as I think *Sons and Lovers*,
carefully read, reveals.

tion. Apart from artistic method, it is not Art that the young
man is studying, but the State of Soul of the great old artist,
so that he may understand his own soul and gain a reconciliation between the aspiration and the resistant.   [*P* 478]

This is personal, but subjective only in a limited sense. In "Study of
Thomas Hardy," from which this passage is taken, young Lawrence
feels his way into his master's state of soul neither by means of rapt
contemplation nor by means of rhapsody but by erecting standards,
by conceptualizing and thus objectifying as criticism the forces active
in the artist's soul. In its effect this work is far more than a personal
encounter; it establishes an intellectual framework and employs a
complex method by means of which Hardy's art is submitted to
analysis.[7]

It is true, particularly in the letters of the 1914–16 period, that
Lawrence liked to trace the inadequacies of an art to an inadequacy
in the soul of the artist. Thus, "I think Crosland's *Sonnets* are objectionable—he is a nasty person" (*L* 178). Or, "the spirit of the thing
[Lascelles Abercrombie's *End of the World*] . . . seems mean and
rather vulgar. . . . What is the matter with the man? There's something wrong with his soul" (*L* 194). And he told Edward Marsh that
he felt his own poetry was improving, "not because I consciously
attend to rhythms, but because I am no longer so criss-crossy in myself" (*L* 135). The quality of the art followed from the quality of the
life, in Lawrence's mind. But whatever genetic theory of art he enter-
tained—and this one is not contemptible—his actual study of soul
includes concrete, relevant perceptions. Here is the full statement of
his attack on Abercrombie:

> And it is no good your telling me Lascelles' *End of the World*
> is great, because it isn't. There are some fine bits of rhetoric,
> as there always are in Abercrombie. But oh, the spirit of the
> thing altogether seems mean and rather vulgar. When I re-
> member H. G. Wells' *Country of the Blind,* with which this

7. This aspect of Lawrence's criticism has been obscured by the quoting
out of context of his arresting remark: "I always say, my motto is 'Art for my
sake.' " As the context makes clear, this means "If I want to write, I write—
and if I don't want to, I won't" (*L* 86). That is, it refers only to his own procedure in composition, not to appreciation as a private experience or to
appreciation at all.

poem of Abercrombie's had got associated beforehand in my mind, then I see how beautiful is Wells' conception, and how paltry this other. Why, why, in God's name, is Abercrombie messing about with Yokels and Cider and runaway wives? No, but it is bitterly disappointing. He who loves *Paradise Lost* must don the red nose and rough-spun cloak of Masefield and Wilfrid. And you encourage it—it is too bad. Abercrombie, if he does anything, surely ought to work upon rather noble and rather chill subjects. I hate and detest his ridiculous imitation yokels and all the silly hash of his bucolics; I loathe his rather nasty efforts at cruelty, like the wrapping of frogs in paper and putting them for cartwheels to crush; I detest his irony with its claptrap solution of everything being that which it seemeth not; and I hate that way of making what Meredith called Cockney metaphors:—moons like a white cat and meteors like a pike fish. And nearly all of this seems to me an Abercrombie turning cheap and wicked. What is the matter with the man? There's something wrong with his soul.   [*L* 194]

Lawrence may abuse the man and the work, but in seeing them in relation to a larger whole, he expands both. He opens horizons, despite the enormous presence in his criticism of his own personality, or perhaps because his personality is so fully identified with his understanding. If we accept Lawrence's definition of the real subjectivist critic as the critic who gives us the impression that he is looking in a mirror,[8] then I think he makes good his claim not to be one. Martin Turnell, reflecting on Remy de Gourmont's celebrated maxim, "The great effort of any sincere man is to erect his personal impressions into laws," comments that this can only be done if one "possesses a body of principles which will give them weight and coherence." He adds that this body of principles "need not be a formal philosophy, but only a large and generous conception of man's nature and destiny."[9] This indicates simply but clearly both a major dilemma of the Romantic critic and Lawrence's way out of it.

There is, of course, a danger for the literary critic with a doctrine (especially for so earnest a teacher as Lawrence), the danger of being doctrinaire, of basing even aesthetic judgments on moral principles.

8. Cited by Richard Aldington in his Introduction to *Selected Essays of D. H. Lawrence* (Baltimore, 1954), p. 9.
9. Turnell, *Dublin Review*, 444, 89.

Lawrence usually escaped this danger because he had an instinctive and keen aesthetic judgment and because he was as honest with his aesthetic reactions as with his moral ones, the sincerity of Lawrence the ideologue being all the more impressive for this reason. Pronounced as were his moral biases, he did not allow them to distort "the sincere statement of the aesthetic and emotional reaction." He found in Fenimore Cooper the germ of a new consciousness, in Hawthorne only a satire on the old one, but he did not rank Cooper over Hawthorne as an *artist*. Cooper, he noted, presents the new idea as wish-fulfillment—i.e. glossily; Hawthorne is more profound, giving us the real undercurrent of tension in American life (S 60, 93).

Or consider his reaction to Galsworthy's story "The Apple Tree," the theme of which might be described as the destruction of simple, natural love by civilized social values. This theme would fit very nicely into the Lawrencean view of things; it is, after all, evident in *Lady Chatterley's Lover,* which was being written at the same time that he commented on Galsworthy's story. But, with a humor that reflects his poise, he sees quickly and penetratingly its unconscious insincerity:

> One of the funniest stories is *The Apple Tree.* The young man finds, at a lonely Devon farm, a little Welsh farm-girl who, being a Celt and not a Saxon, at once falls for the Galsworthian hero. The young gentleman, in the throes of narcissistic love for his marvellous self, falls for the maid because she has fallen so abjectly for him. She doesn't call him "My King," not being Wellsian; she only says: "I can't live away from you. Do what you like with me. Only let me come with you!" The proper prostitutional announcement!
>
> For this, of course, a narcissistic young gentleman just down from Oxford falls at once. Ensues a grand pa-assion. He goes to buy her a proper frock to be carried away in, meets a college friend with a young lady sister, has jam for tea and stays the night, and the grand pa-assion has died a natural death by the time he spreads the marmalade on his bread. He has returned to his own class. But to fill the cup of his vanity, the maid drowns herself. It is funny that maids only seem to do it for these narcissistic young gentlemen who, looking in the pool for their own image, desire the added satisfaction of seeing the face of drowned Ophelia there as well; saving them the necessity

of taking the narcissus plunge in person. We have gone one better than the myth. Narcissus, in Mr. Galsworthy, doesn't drown himself. He asks Ophelia, or Megan, kindly to drown herself instead. And in this fiction she actually does! And he feels so *wonderful* about it! [*P* 546]

Lawrence had instinctive good taste. One must add, of course, that he was almost indifferent to the matter of taste, that he was primarily interested in the moral values of literature, and that he even expressed his aesthetic reactions in morally charged language. But it is possible to demonstrate that he recognized a distinction between aesthetic and moral judgment. Consider the following: "I can see all the poetry at the *back* of your verse—but there isn't much inside the lines. It's the rhythm and the sound that don't penetrate the blood" (*L* 72). Davies' *Nature Poems* "seem so thin, one can hardly feel them at all" (*L* 174). "Gissing hasn't enough energy, enough sanguinity, to capture me. But I esteem him a good deal" (*CL* 94). Edward Garnett's *Jeanne d'Arc* "seems to me a human record rather than a play, and I don't know how to criticize it at all. . . . When the figures are ready-made in dry material, I should think it's the devil to breathe life into them" (*L* 84). "I send you the *Spoon River Anthology*. It is good, but too static, always stated, not really art" (*CL* 431). "I was reading Aretino's *Ragionamenti*—sometimes amusing, but not *created* enough" (*L* 717). These are fundamentally aesthetic judgments, based on the criteria: sufficiency of energy, sufficiency of imagination.

In contrast, consider the following: "Petronius is straight and above-board. Whatever he does, he doesn't try to degrade and dirty the pure mind in him. But Dostoievsky, mixing God and Sadism, he is foul" (*L* 313–14). "I hate Strindberg—he seems unnatural, forced, a bit indecent—a bit wooden, like Ibsen, a bit skin-erupty" (*L* 66). "Yeats seems awfully queer stuff to me now—as if he wouldn't bear touching" (*CL* 168). "I'm nearly through Mark Rutherford. How good he is!—so just, so harmonious" (*L* 80–81). These are primarily moral judgments, based on the criteria: harmony of mind and body, harmony of self and world. The praise probably implies a degree of aesthetic merit, but the censure does not necessarily imply aesthetic inadequacy.

Richard Aldington confuses the issue when he tells us, "It is the fact that among his contemporaries Lawrence chiefly admired insignificant writers, and had poor literary judgment."[1] Lawrence's admiration for lesser contemporaries is usually based on moral grounds and is otherwise qualified, as are his attacks on major contemporaries. It is one of the marks of Lawrence's taste that he did not quarrel deeply with second-rate writers. Where comparative aesthetic judgments are in order, as in group reviews, he is quite sensible, seeing, for example, that Dos Passos and Hemingway are better writers than Carl Van Vechten and Walter White.

If we can recognize Lawrence's aesthetic judgment as instinctively sound, we can more easily deal with Eliot's distrust of the Inner Light, for Eliot is in effect asking how one can trust one's own instincts to be true. He seems to be attacking Lawrence less for the truth of his conclusions than for unconscious insincerity, for "drawing the wrong

---

1. Certainly the evidence Aldington offers for his "fact" is not convincing. He writes, "Lawrence seems to have been surprised at the willingness of editors to publish Murry, and I find very little evidence that he appreciated Katherine Mansfield" (*Portrait of a Genius But . . .* [London, 1950], p. 182). Nothing in the published record supports this opinion. "Katherine Mansfield was not a great genius. She had a charming gift and a finely cultivated one. But not more, and to try, as you [Murry] do, to make it more, is to do her no true service" (quoted in Catherine Carswell, *The Savage Pilgrimage* [London, 1932], p. 198. That seems fair enough, just and exact. As for remarks on Murry's work, the following is typical: "Murry's *Keats* was quite good—many thanks—but oh heaven, so die away—the text might be: Oh, lap up Shakespeare till you've cleaned the dish, and you may hope to swoon into raptures and die an early but beautiful death at 25" (Moore, *The Intelligent Heart,* p. 347). It is a characteristic squib, the merit briefly acknowledged, the moral implications assaulted.

Diana Trilling makes a similar charge:

> She [Frieda] had no taste, as we mean the exercise of artistic judgment. But then neither had Lawrence; Lawrence never thought of art in terms of taste any more than he thought of art in terms of permanence. The value for Lawrence of a created work lay not in its lastingness or in its conformity to esthetic standards but in its rightness at the moment for its creator, in its usefulness as a form of personal communication. He cared just as much about his painting as about his writing and he wasn't a very good painter.   [*SL* xvii]

The statement is glibly inexact. Having no taste is not the same thing as not thinking of art in terms of taste. The question of permanence *did* concern him, as I shall show in the next chapter. As for his painting, the record shows that, although he cared for it, he did not rate it high critically (see "Making Pictures," in *Assorted Articles*).

conclusions in his conscious mind from insights which came to him from below consciousness."[2] This is only another way of framing his basic charge that Lawrence lacked the faculty of self-criticism.

But to be honest as Lawrence was honest requires self-criticism and self-awareness. As Leavis pointed out, we should not be misled by the absence of hesitation and self-doubt in his manner.[3] An essential self-criticism is apparent in Lawrence's freedom to contradict himself, to change his mind or shift his ground from work to work—as he does, for instance, in the revisions of *Studies*—without calling attention to the fact. It is apparent in what is best called his tact: his sense of the appropriate tone to adopt for the subject at hand, his directness in confronting issues, his knowing what not to say, and his choice of quotation (his essay on *Moby Dick* is an excellent example of criticism conducted largely by means of apt quotation). The curious fact is that Eliot himself has praised most of these qualities in other connections, but he seems unable to find them illustrated in so radically individualistic a writer as Lawrence.

We may admit that sincerity alone has its pitfalls. Unless combined with a sense of humor, it can easily result in the oversolemn manner of Tolstoi's *What Is Art* and some of Ruskin's literary criticism. (Tolstoi and Ruskin, for example, averred that a bad man could not be a good artist, whereas Lawrence characteristically took a more subtle and ironic view, noting that a man *as a man* might be profligate but *as an artist* must be "pure in spirit"—*AA* 169.) Eliot not surprisingly finds Lawrence lacking also in a sense of humor.[4] But Lawrence was fully aware of the risks of sincerity, commenting, apropos of Frederick Rolfe, who had fallen "head over heels in deadly earnest": "A man must keep his earnestness nimble, to escape ridicule" (*P* 327). We should not expect to find in Lawrence, any more than in Blake, the kind of self-directed irony and self-conscious qualification that we find in Eliot. Both were too passionate and too earnest. But they were men of tough intellect and knew how to keep

2. From T. S. Eliot's Foreword to William Tiverton, *D. H. Lawrence and Human Existence* (New York, 1951), p. vii.
3. "The Wild Untutored Phoenix," in *The Importance of Scrutiny*, ed. with intro. by Eric Bentley (New York, 1948), p. 340.
4. *After Strange Gods*, p. 62.

their earnestness nimble.[5] They had critical tact: they were aware of the effect of their expression on their audience; they knew how to use humor to maintain their balance; their touch was deft, neat, and quick. These qualities in Lawrence are most apparent in his reviews, and it may prove helpful to quote from a typical one at some length. Here is the first half or so of his review of an American verse anthology (1922):

> "It is not merely an assembly of verse, but the spiritual record of an entire people."—This from the wrapper of *A Second Comtemporary Verse Anthology.* The spiritual record of an entire people sounds rather impressive. This book as a matter of fact is a collection of pleasant verse, neat and nice and easy as eating candy.
>
> Naturally any collection of contemporary verse in any country at any time is bound to be more or less a box of candy. Days of Horace, days of Milton, days of Whitman, it would be pretty much the same, more or less a box of candy. Would it be at the same time the spiritual record of an entire people? Why not? If we had a good representative anthology of the poetry of Whitman's day, and if it contained two poems by Whitman, then it would be a fairly true spiritual record of the American people of that day. As if the whole nation had whispered or chanted its inner experience into the horn of a gramophone.
>
> And the bulk of the whisperings and murmurings would be candy: sweet nothings, tender trifles, amusing things. For of such is the bulk of the spiritual experience of any entire people.
>
> The Americans have always been good at "occasional" verse. Sixty years ago they were very good indeed: making their little

5. In an engaging imaginary dialogue between himself as poet and an apotheosized interlocutor, later revealed as Lawrence himself, Karl Shapiro admits that, although Lawrence's poetic craft seems to him inferior to that of the leading poets of our century, his poetry satisfies him more because of its greater sincerity and honesty. When these words prompt his interlocutor to introduce the name of William Carlos Williams for consideration, Shapiro says, yes, but "Williams lets me down in another way. He is *too* sincere. . . . Williams' refusal to be anything *but* true to the language . . . becomes just another . . . stylistic obsession." Shapiro does not go on to explain how Lawrence's sincerity escapes this danger, but I think his nimbleness or wit has much to do with it. See Shapiro's "The Unemployed Magician," in Moore, *Miscellany,* pp. 378–95.

joke against themselves and their century. Today there are fewer jokes. There are also fewer footprints in the sands of time. Life is still earnest, but a little less real. And the soul has left off asserting that dust it isn't nor to dust returneth. The spirit of verse prefers now a "composition salad" of fruits and sensations, in a cooked mayonnaise of sympathy. Odds and ends of feeling smoothed into unison by some prevailing sentiment.

> My face is wet with the rain
> But my heart is warm to the core . . .

Or you can call it a box of chocolate candies. Let me offer you a sweet! Isn't everything candy?

> There be none of beauty's daughters
> With a magic like thee—
> And like music on the waters
> Is thy sweet voice to me.

Is that candy? Then what about this?

> But you are a girl and run
>   Fresh bathed and warm and sweet,
> After the flying ball
>   On little sandalled feet.

One of those two fragments is a classic. And one is a scrap from the contemporary spiritual record.

> The river boat had loitered down its way,
> The ropes were coiled, and business for the day
> Was done—
>
> Now fades the glimmering landscape on the sight,
> And all the air a solemn stillness holds;
> Save where—

Two more bits. Do you see any intrinsic difference between them? After all, the one *means* as much as the other. And what is there in the mere stringing together of words?

For some mysterious reason, there is everything.

> When lilacs last in the dooryard bloomed—

It is a string of words, but it makes me prick my innermost ear. So do I prick my ear to: "Fly low, vermilion dragon." But

the next line: "With the moon horns," makes me lower that
same inward ear once more, in indifference.
There is an element of danger in all new utterance . . .
[*P* 322–23]

There is much to praise in this: the quick, unforced penetration to
an issue of significance—the more remarkable because the subject does
not seem to have seized Lawrence's interest at once; the deft posing
of lines from Byron and Gray against the skillfully excerpted mediocre
verse of the anthology; the evident sense of fact, which Lawrence,
"an ignorant man" with no "intellectual and social training," is supposed to lack; the flexible rhythm of the piece, more naturally responsive to the interaction of life and literature than the more labored,
calculated rhythms of most reviews; and, finally, what Leavis has
called "the lively ironic humour," which guards the critic against
breaking a butterfly upon a wheel, and which, as Leavis says, is at the
same time so "free of snobbishness, pose and affectation."[6]
Leavis has also described the critic Lawrence as "completely disinterested" and "radically free from egotism,"[7] and the description,
however strange it seems in reference to so partisan a writer, is just.
For Lawrence's literary criticism was, to an unusual degree, uninfluenced by hope of personal gain, by the desire to please or to create a
flattering image of himself, or even by his own intellectual biases.
I would qualify the positiveness of Leavis' judgment, however, in
two rather minor ways. The *tone* of some of Lawrence's opinions does
not seem quite uninfluenced by contemporary currents of taste. A
certain measure of his harshness toward Dostoevsky, for example, is
probably to be explained as a reaction to the immense prestige which
the latter had suddenly acquired in Lawrence's day, particularly among
members of his circle,[8] and a certain measure of his enthusiasm for

6. In Bentley, *The Importance of Scrutiny*, p. 339.
7. Ibid., pp. 342, 339. Note also Vivante's eulogy: "Nobody was less influenced by extrinsic aims, either theological or moral, and by egocentric
interests, or preconceptions of any kind" (*A Philosophy of Potentiality*,
pp. 100–01).
8. Edward Garnett and Middleton Murry wrote books on Dostoevsky;
Constance Garnett and S. Koteliansky translated him; everyone was talking
about him. Frank Swinnerton, in *The Georgian Literary Scene* (New York,
1934), notes that "it would be hard to exaggerate the impression made upon
young readers [in England] in 1912 by the appearance of *The Brothers
Karamazov*" (p. 238).

the classic Americans is probably to be explained as a response to their relatively meager reputations. But there can be no question that his judgments in both cases were essentially sincere and disinterested.[9] Secondly, I see Lawrence as a man not beyond the temptation to compromise, but one who can't help being honest in spite of it. This is the man who set out in *The Lost Girl* to write a potboiler, but made it a serious and characteristic novel before he had finished (see *L* 427, 497); who wanted to "castrate" *Lady Chatterley's Lover* for the public market, but had to leave it as it was ("A Propos" 91).

This temptation to compromise, when it finds expression in his critical practice, provides interesting illustration of his peculiarly compulsive honesty, even if it somewhat mars the criticism. I am thinking of those few reviews and prefaces which Lawrence volunteered on behalf of authors who were personal friends but unremarkable writers. The conflict of loyalties produced a few curious results, an example of which is worth a moment's notice.

In reviewing Walter Wilkinson's *The Peep Show,* a book praising the simple joys of life as experienced by a traveling puppeteer, Lawrence writes: "The very banalities at last have the effect of the *mot juste.* . . . Owing to the true limpidity and vicelessness of the author, ordinariness becomes almost vivid. The book . . . has therefore its own touch of realization of the tragedy of human futility: the futility even of ordinariness." And: "Call it a human document, call it literature, I don't know the difference" (*P* 373). Each of these remarks is characteristic enough—the first recalling Lawrence's method of saving a book by showing it to be unconsciously satirical, the second reminding us of his precept that art is no more than life—

9. A further qualification probably ought to be added to this one, for I do think there is some truth in Richard Aldington's assertion that Lawrence "feared strong influences" (*Portrait of a Genius But* . . . , p. 181): hence his ungenerous antagonism to some writers with whom he had much in common, such as Rousseau, the English Romantic poets, Nietzsche, and Shaw. But the objections he makes to them are fundamental to his whole world view. And Lawrence could be quite generous in acknowledging the help he got from scholarly books: e.g. Frazer's *Golden Bough,* John Burnet's *Early Greek Philosophy,* Mrs. Jenner's *Christ in Art,* Jane Harrison's *Art and Ritual* (*L* 149, 163, 476; *F* 54). In fact, to read some of these books is to realize how indifferent he could be to alien intellectual objectives when he was finding information he could make use of.

but both have here a rather defensive, hollow ring: "almost vivid" and a "touch of realization" are equivocal phrases, and usually he *does* recognize a distinction between a human record and art, between what is merely stated and what is created. There is another voice running throughout the review, stronger and clearer and less fettered. He quotes from Wilkinson: "It is an exquisite pleasure to find oneself so suddenly in the sweet morning air, to tumble out of bed, to clamber over a stone wall and scramble across some rushy dunes down to the untrodden seashore, there to take one's bath in the lively breakers." And comments:

> It is almost a masterpiece of clichés. . . . It is what the "ordinary" young man who is "really nice" does write. You have to have something vicious in you to be a creative writer. It is the something vicious, old-adamish, incompatible with the "ordinary" world, inside a man, which gives an edge to his awareness, and makes it impossible for him to talk of a "bath in the lively breakers."

The review concludes in this latter vein: "All the reader can say, at the end of this songful, cheerful book is: 'God save me from the nice, ordinary people. . . . God save me from being "nice"' " (P 372–76).[1]

The point is that, even if Lawrence was sometimes an undisciplined writer, his trust in the Inner Light was not incompatible with a real

---

1. A similar example is Lawrence's introduction to Harry Crosby's book of verse, *Chariot in the Sun* (P 255–62). The first half of it was written and published earlier as an independent essay entitled "Chaos in Poetry" (in *Exchanges*, 1929), and is a straightforward, vigorous statement on the theme: "The essential value of poetry is that it makes a new effort of attention, and 'discovers' a new world within the known world." But with the question, "What, then, of *Chariot in the Sun?*" a new tone seems to enter the essay. "It is useless to quote fragments," writes Lawrence, having quoted two that are not impressive, but he goes on to quote more fragments for several pages. He defends the line, "sthhe fous on ssu eod," on the grounds: "In a world overloaded with shallow 'sense,' I can bear a page of nonsense, just for a pause." And, after a few more fragments, he exclaims: "What does it matter if half the time a poet fails in his effort at expression! The failures make it real." This fretful defense attests, I think, to the fact that he knows he is claiming more for Crosby's verse than his sincere feeling warrants. It is one of the few times that Lawrence's sense of knowing when to stop seems to desert him, and it is noteworthy that Crosby himself suggested the introduction be truncated (see L 736).

kind of self-criticism, with an ability to sense both the sincerity and the effectiveness of his own expression. That he might sometimes exceed himself and look a little foolish was a price he was willing to pay.

A consideration of Lawrence's salient characteristics as a critic would not be complete without more particular mention of his almost uncanny directness, much like the naked force or "terrifying honesty" that Eliot found in Blake. Leavis and Huxley justly compare Lawrence to Blake for his ability to know so surely what he was interested in.[2] There is, of course, an obverse side to this strength, which Leavis hardly acknowledges: the partiality of an exclusive point of view. One would never guess from reading Lawrence that Shakespeare wrote anything but tormented tragedy or that Dickens and Shaw were interested in anything but manners and customs. But his interest, when aroused, penetrates so directly to fundamentals that his criticism often gives the impression of being extraordinarily inclusive. His witty little synopses of Hardy's early novels, of the Leatherstocking Tales, of *The Blithedale Romance,* are more substantive interpretations than many full essays on the same subjects. Still more impressive is a letter of 1916 to Middleton Murry and Katherine Mansfield, presenting "some notes on Dostoievsky." It constitutes a firm, richly suggestive outline for a full-length book, and the passage is worth quoting in its entirety:

> I'll write you some "notes" on Dostoievsky—you can translate them into your own language, if they interest you.
> 1. He has a fixed will, a mania to be infinite, to be God.
> 2. Within this will, his activity is twofold:
>   (a) To be self-less, a pure Christian, to live in the outer whole, the social whole, the self-less whole, the universal consciousness.
>   (b) To be a pure, absolute self, all-devouring and all-consuming.
> That is the main statement about him.
> His desire to achieve the sensual, all-devouring consummation comes out in Dmitri Karamazov, and Rogozhin, and, not so clearly, in Stavrogin.

---

2. Leavis, *For Continuity* (Cambridge, 1931), pp. 122 ff. Aldous Huxley, Introduction to *The Letters of D. H. Lawrence,* ed. A. Huxley (London, 1932), p. xi.

His desire for the spiritual, turn-the-other-cheek consummation, comes out in the Idiot himself, in Alyosha, partly in Stavrogin.

There is the third type, which represents pure unemotional *will:* this is the third Karamazov brother, and Pyotr Stepanovitch, and the young secretary man at whose house the Idiot first lodges—he who is going to marry the young woman —Gavril, is [that] his name? The whole point of Dostoievsky lies in the fact of his fixed will that the individual ego, the achieved I, the conscious entity, shall be infinite, God-like, and absolved of relation, i.e. free.

I like *The Idiot* best. The Idiot is showing the last stage of Christianity, of becoming purely self-less, of becoming disseminated out into a pure, absolved consciousness. This is the Christian ecstasy, when I become so transcendentally superconscious that I am bodiless, that the universe is my consciousness. This is the little Idiot prince. It is the ecstasy of being devoured in the body, like the Christian lamb, and of transcendence in the consciousness, the spirit.

Karamazov is concerned with the last stages—not nearly so far gone—of sensuality, of unconscious experience purely within the self. I reach such a pitch of dark sensual ecstasy that I seem to be, I myself, the universal night that has swallowed everything. I become universal, the universal devouring darkness. This is Dmitri Karamazov. This was Dostoievsky's real desire, to obtain this sensual ecstasy of universality. This is why Father Zossima bowed to Dmitri—Zossima is pure Christian, self-less, universal in the social whole. Dead, he stinks.

He was sadish because his *will* was fixed on the social virtues, because he felt himself *wrong* in his sensual seekings. Therefore he was cruel, he tortured himself and others, and *goûtait* the tortures.

The Christian ecstasy leads to imbecility (*The Idiot*). The sensual ecstasy leads to universal murder: for mind, the acme of sensual ecstasy, lies in *devouring* the other, like a tiger drinking blood. But the full sensual ecstasy is never reached except by Rogozhin in murdering Nastasya. It is nipped in the last stages by the *will,* the social will. When the police stripped Dmitri Karamazov naked, they killed in him the quick of his being, his lust for the sensual ecstasy. [This was written, by the way, before Lawrence's own experience with the army medical examiners.]

The men who represent will, the pure mental, social, rational, absolved will, Ivan Karamazov, and Pyotr Stepanovitch, and Gavril, they represent the last stages of our social development, the human being become mechanical, absolved from all relation. When Stepan talks with the devil, the devil is a decayed social gentleman—only that. The mechanical social forms and aspirations and ideals, I suppose, are the devil.

The women are not important. They are the mere echoes and objectives of the men. They *desire* the sensual ecstasy, all of them, even the cripple in *The Possessed* ("My hawk, my eagle," she says to Stavrogin). They have the opposite wild love for purity, self-lessness, extreme Christianity. And they are *all* ultimately bound to the social convention—all the "great" women, that is. The cripple in *The Possessed,* and Nastasya Filipovna, and Dmitri Karamazov's women, these desire only the sensual ecstasy: but all the while they admit themselves the inferior of the other Christian ecstasy: which is the social ecstasy.

They are great parables, the novels, but false art. They are only parables. All the people are fallen angels—even the dirtiest scrubs. This I cannot stomach. People are not fallen angels, they are merely people. But Dostoievsky used them all as theological or religious units, they are all terms of divinity, like Christ's "Sower went forth to sow," and Bunyan's *Pilgrim's Progress.* They are bad art, false truth.   [L 325–27]

In sum, we may call Lawrence himself the ideal Lawrencean critic: emotionally very alive, intellectually capable and skillful in essential logic, and morally very honest. To an extent, these qualities simply characterize a good as opposed to a mediocre critic, but they are also distinctively Lawrencean. They indicate a criticism remarkable for its independence, its economy and force, and its sincerity—a sincerity that reveals the critic's disinterestedness and self-awareness. Lawrence's profound trust in his own vital and sincere emotion is the basis of a criticism that is partial, passionate, and political, but neither inaccessibly subjective nor lacking in discrimination and taste.

Clearly it would be inappropriate to present Lawrence as a model formal critic. "Art," he told a friend, using the word in the sense of craft or technique, "does not interest me. Only the spiritual content" (*CB I* 293). (When he referred to Dostoevsky's "bad art" at the end of the letter quoted above, he of course meant art in an opposite sense: spiritual content or spiritual truth.) And as we have seen, he dismissed "all the critical twiddle-twaddle about style and form" as "mere impertinence and mostly dull jargon." This sweeping dismissal, however, is somewhat misleading, for, as we shall see in the following chapter, he had his own ideas of style and form. And in order fully to appreciate the fact that Lawrence was not struggling toward an aesthetic out of ignorance or incapacity, we must remind ourselves that he was, when he cared to be, a first-rate practical critic.

Poe, he writes, "seeks a sensation from every phrase or object, and the effect is vulgar" (*SM* 113). His style

> seems to me a meretricious affair. "Her marble hand" and "the elasticity of her footfall" seem more like chairsprings and mantlepieces than a human creature. . . .
> All Poe's style, moreover, has this mechanical quality, as his poetry has a mechanical rhythm. He never sees anything in terms of life, almost always in terms of matter, jewels, marble, etc.—or in terms of force, scientific.   [*S* 78]

Of Verga's stories in *Cavelleria Rusticana:*

> The transitions are too abrupt. All is over in a gasp whereas a story like "La Lupa" covers at least several years of time. . . . We need more looseness. . . . A great deal of the meaning of life and of art lies in the apparently dull spaces, the pauses, the unimportant passages. They are truly passages, the places of passing over. . . . "La Lupa" may be a masterpiece of concision, but it is hardly a masterpiece of narration.[3]   [*P* 247]

3. The aesthetic critic will as a rule try to show how the style and form of a work support, or fail to support, the author's apparent intention. Lawrence *seems* to ignore this procedure (seems not to ask himself, for instance, whether Poe's inorganic imagery and mechanical rhythms or Verga's abrupt transitions have artistic relevance), because he is hostile to the apparent intention. But he understands it perfectly well, and when or insofar as he can discover an intention of which he does approve, he will relate style and form to it. In *Studies* I, for instance, where he views Poe's inorganicism more appreciatively, he speaks of his style as "a slow method of musing abstraction . . . subtle, accurate . . . and careful," fitting his purpose, which was "scientific progress in sensation" (*SM* 109–10). And in the same essay in which he criticizes

Consider Lawrence as a practical critic of poetry. In 1910 he wrote to Rachel Annand Taylor, a poet of some reputation in his Eastwood circle: "I don't like your arrangement of vowel sounds: it is not emotional enough—too intellectual. One can get good Swinburnian consonant music by taking thought, but never Shakespearean vowel-loveliness, in which the emotion of the piece flows" (*SL* 5). To Edward Marsh a few years later he explained and illustrated the concept of stock responses, *avant la lettre:*

> And now I've got to quarrel with you about the Ralph Hodgson poem: because I think it is banal in utterance. The feeling is there, right enough—but not in itself, only represented. It's like "I asked for bread, and he gave me a penny." Only here and there is the least touch of personality in the poem: it is the currency of poetry, not poetry itself. . . . Look:
>
> > the ruby's and the rainbow's song
> > the nightingale's—all three
>
> There's the emotion in the rhythm, but it's a loose emotion, inarticulate, common—the words are mere currency. It is exactly like a man who feels very strongly for a beggar, and gives him a sovereign. "Oh, I do want to give you this emotion," cries Hodgson, "I do." And so he takes out his poetic purse, and gives you a handful of cash, and feels very strongly, even a bit sentimentally over it.
>
> > ——the sky was lit
> > The sky was stars all over it,
> > I stood, I knew not why
>
> No one should say "I knew not why" any more. It is as meaningless as "yours truly" at the end of a letter.   [*L* 152]

It is worth noting that both of these latter passages and in fact most of Lawrence's practical criticisms are to be found in his letters, especially the early ones. Throughout his career, and increasingly as he developed his position, he seems to have regarded questions of

---

Verga's abruptness, he also grants it, in relation to a deeper intention, an appropriateness. It represents the attempt to convey "the emotional mind," which "makes curious swoops and circles. It touches the point of pain or interest, then sweeps away again in a cycle, coils round and approaches the point of pain or interest" (*P* 249-50).

craft as matter fit merely for shoptalk. In criticism designed for publication, his interest lies elsewhere. He does not totally ignore the twiddle-twaddle of style and form even there. In almost every review he makes some comment concerning craft but, as a rule, parenthetically, in a kind of prescript or postscript. For instance, he criticizes banality of expression (as we saw in his review of *The Peep Show*), pomposity of style (see his reviews of Stuart Sherman's *Americans,* Cunninghame Graham's *Pedro de Valdivia,* and Eric Gill's *Art Nonsense and Other Essays*), affected modernism (see reviews of Leo Shestov's *All Things Are Possible* and W. C. Williams' *In the American Grain*) and even accuracy of translation (see again his review of *Pedro de Valdivia*); he notes flaws of structure (in Marmaduke Pickthall's *Saïd the Fisherman* and Baron Corvo's *Hadrian the Seventh*). But as far as Lawrence was concerned, "If an author rouses my deeper sympathy, he can have as many faults as he likes" (P 336). The Lawrence who admired Fenimore Cooper would not have objected to a listing of the latter's literary offenses; he would have shrugged and turned his attention elsewhere. Interestingly, in manuscript jottings preparatory to his hostile study of Galsworthy, Lawrence makes peppery rhetorical criticisms which are omitted in the published draft.[4]

At the end of his reviews and prefaces he characteristically turns outward from the book or literary issue in question toward our predicament and prospects as social beings. For example, at the conclusion of his essay on Galsworthy, having exposed the sentimentalism of *The Forsyte Saga,* he writes, "But if the sticky mess gets much deeper, even the little Forsytes won't be able to bob up any more. They'll be smothered in their own slime along with everything else. Which is a comfort" (P 534). Or, concluding his examination of Verga's *Mastro-don Gesualdo,* in which he held up for admiration Verga's ability to create wholesomely naïve characters, he remarks, "Whether

4. " 'The moon at her curve's summit floated at peace on the blue surface of the sky, a great closed water-lily' (water-lilies don't have a curve's summit— even if a curve itself has one) 'And Martin saw through the trees scimitar-shaped reeds clustering black along the pool's shore' (reeds don't cluster—he must have jerked his head very suddenly from the moon's summit to the pond) 'All about him the may-flowers were alight (why alight?) It was such a night as makes dreams real and turns reality to dreams.' clap trap!" (Quoted in Tedlock, *Manuscripts,* p. 170.)

[Gesualdo] would have been any the better for waking up to himself, who knows!" (*P* 231)

Lawrence had no intention of letting art transfigure all that dread. The need for a new society and a new consciousness too urgently engaged him. "One day he damned me heartily," one of his friends tells us, "for being, like my generation, drunk with Dostoievsky. I tried to defend myself. 'But Dostoievsky's a genius! Don't you think so too?' 'That isn't the point,'" Lawrence is reported to have said, "'You're all making a mistake. You all think he is concerned with God. Can't you see that his only concern, his only interest, is in *sin?*'" (*CB I* 293). Or consider two typical, informal reactions to books—one early, one late—as illustrations of the kind of overriding moral passion he brought to the criticism of literature. In 1912 he wrote to Edward Garnett concerning a character in a play (*Lords and Masters*) that Garnett had written: "Mrs. Henderson—I mean the young one—I could shoot her. She is typical of all that is exasperating in women. She is most abominably true" (*L* 19). And to Aldous Huxley, in 1929:

> I have read *Point Counter Point* with a heart sinking through
> my bootsoles and a rising admiration. I do think you've shown
> the truth, perhaps the last truth, about you and your generation,
> with really fine courage. . . . But . . . what a state! if you can
> only palpitate to murder, suicide, and rape, in their various
> degrees—and you state plainly that it is so—*caro,* however
> are we going to live through the days? . . . Why do men only
> thrill to a woman who'll rape them? All I want to do to your
> Lucy is smack her across the mouth.   [*L* 757–58]

Secondarily, he praises the artistic effectiveness of these works. But that isn't the point. The point, his primary interest, is the truth they reveal in terms of his own burning vision of man and society. He could admire the artist who had the courage to expose error and yet rage against him (or against his characters, insofar as they could not be saved by him or from him) for not summoning the courage to rouse his vision, on behalf of his culture, toward greater freedom and more abundant life.

The real subtlety and complexity of Lawrence's literary criticism, then, lies not in its concern for artistry as such but for art in relation to morality. An examination of his theory of art, his aesthetic, will take us to the heart of this intricate and essential relation.

3

The Aesthetic

In a review of *Death in Venice,* written as early as 1912, Lawrence made a statement which will prove a useful starting point for a discussion of his aesthetic:

> It seems to me this craving for form is the outcome, not of artistic conscience, but of a certain attitude to life. For form is not a personal thing like style. It is impersonal like logic. And just as the school of Alexander Pope was logical in its expressions, so it seems to me the school of Flaubert is, as it were, logical in its aesthetic form. "Nothing outside the definite line of the book," is a maxim. But can the human mind fix absolutely any definite line of action for a living being?   [*P* 308]

A true style, then, would be personal. In a foreword to *Women in Love* Lawrence wrote, "In point of style, fault is often found with the continual, slightly modified repetition. The only answer is that it is natural to the author." If a writer lets himself go, as he should, his style will reflect his temperament and bias. "To be honest in writing," he advised a friend, "one has to write from some point of view, and leave all other aspects, from all remaining points of view, to be conjectured. One can't write without feeling—and feeling is bias."[1]

1. From a letter to Mabel Luhan, quoted in her book *Lorenzo in Taos* (New York, 1932), p. 260.

Hence he was critical of styles that were impartial, dispassionate, objective. Impersonality or lack of attitude was unnatural to a writer and in that sense dishonest.[2]

True form, on the other hand, would be impersonal. Lawrence is a little confusing when he writes first that form "is impersonal like logic" and then that the school of Flaubert is "logical in its aesthetic form," for he intends a contrast here between true and false impersonality, between spontaneity and self-consciousness. Flaubert—like Joyce, who echoed him on this point, and like Eliot—believed that the artist should efface himself. But according to Lawrence, when the artist effaces himself, "one is far more aware of his interference than when he just goes ahead. . . .[3] Because any self-effacement is . . . self-conscious, and any form of emotional self-consciousness hinders a first-rate artist: though it may help the second-rate" (P 248). One gives one's self away in books, Lawrence believed, and should not be afraid to do so. Self-effacement was neither natural nor honest. So the craving for form was "the outcome, not of artistic conscience, but of a certain attitude to life." Such form would be contrived and willed. It would predetermine events and push them into line according to the artist's personal predilection. Flaubertian form seemed to Lawrence the product of the attitudinizing ego, of personality.

We should not confuse Lawrence's frequent disparagement of self-consciousness and personality with Eliot's. William Tiverton, in *D. H. Lawrence and Human Existence,* compares Lawrence's "one sheds one's sicknesses in books—repeats and presents again one's emotions, to be master of them," to Eliot's "poetry is not a turning

2. This applied to all kinds of writing. Reviewing a book on prohibition to which he conceded some value as scholarship, he jibed, "One wonders if anything should try to be so angelically dispassionate: anything except an adding-up machine" (P 331). And to Trigant Burrow, whose *The Social Basis of Consciousness* he admired: "But do you know, I think you are really more a philosopher, or artist, than a scientist—and that you have a deep *natural* resistance to this scientific jargonizing—which makes your style sometimes so excruciating—whereas the moment you let yourself go, it is perfect to your matter" (L 687–88).

3. A remark of Lionel Trilling's lends support to Lawrence's view: "Flaubert himself never could, despite his own theory, keep himself out of his books; we always know who is there by guessing who it is that is kept out."—*The Liberal Imagination* (New York, 1957) p. 262.

loose of emotion but an escape from emotion, not an expression of personality, but an escape from personality"[4]—and wrongly, I think. The psychologies are different. Lawrence equates personality with ego and mind, Eliot with emotion and feeling. For Lawrence emotion is impersonal and cognitive; for Eliot it is personal and noncognitive —which helps to explain why Lawrence could trust emotion so much and Eliot so little, and perhaps why Eliot found so little evidence of intelligence in Lawrence. Eliot's quarrel with personality is linked with his objection to art as self-expression. For him the mind of the poet transmutes experience into art primarily through its preoccupation with the artistic medium, with form. But Lawrence believed that emotion in conjunction with its own intelligence would achieve a truer form.

Actually, the two differ not so much on the question of the *presence* of intellect in the creative process as on the question of its *role*. The immediate awareness of the emotions by the mind—i.e. self-consciousness—resulted in the kind of irony which Eliot recommended. This is to be distinguished from Lawrencean irony ("Romantic," we may call it), which emerges from the discrepancy between aspiration and fulfillment. For Lawrence the business of the intellect was to prevent interference from the self-conscious ego, the attitudinizing secondary self. The creative emotion must work itself out; the "aspirant" must seek realization, checked only by its intrinsic "resistant." What was required of the artist was not the absence of bias but the suspension of a preconceived end or final determination—that is, a deliberate naïveté, but a naïveté that was necessary if he were to be fully open to experience, to possibility, to life.

Lawrence's view of personality in the creative process must also be distinguished from the view taken by some Romantic critics, though the distinction is a finer one. Keats and Hazlitt, for instance, in formulating the concepts of negative capability and sympathetic identification, stressed the capacity of the artist to lose his personality by identifying himself with the object of contemplation. But in Lawrence's view, the artist (or man—the merging of the two being characteristic of Romantic thought) must neither lose himself in the other nor absorb the other into himself, for unless self and other

4. Tiverton, *Lawrence,* p. 59.

maintain their integrities, true relationship might dissolve. In short, Lawrence proposed a central, or creative, consciousness fluid enough to escape the habits of the mental-social consciousness but integral enough to be capable of normative judgment.

The critic Lawrence is supposed to be a proponent of "expressive form," but R. P. Blackmur's definition of that term, in his challenging and influential essay "D. H. Lawrence and Expressive Form," does not quite correspond to Lawrence's meaning. Blackmur defines it as "the faith . . . that if a thing is only intensely enough felt its mere expression in words will give it satisfactory form, the dogma, in short, that once material becomes words it is its own best form"; and he regards this faith as a "stultifying fallacy."[5] Lawrence does at times lay himself open to such an attack, but much of its relevance is lost when we realize that the "rational" or "objective" form which Blackmur thinks is necessary to avoid "hysteria" simply means traditional form, and that no acknowledgment is made of the fact that individual vision, either in art or in criticism, is capable of creating its own order. According to Lawrence, since the aspirant and resistant "must always meet under fresh conditions, form must always be different. Every work of art has its own form, which has no relation to any other form" (*P* 454).

Blackmur himself gives us the means to defend Lawrence when he writes, "What is expressed in hysteria can never be wholly understood until the original reality is regained either by analysis or the imposition of limits."[6] The establishing of limits for the sake of analysis is Lawrence's habitual procedure. For example, the categories "sensual ecstasy" and "spiritual ecstasy," as used in his letter on Dostoevsky or in *Women in Love,* establish the limits of vital being and the needed conceptual base for the analysis of characters. "Analytical" was the word Lawrence himself used to describe the form of what was becoming *Women in Love* (*L* 111).

Blackmur compares Lawrence unfavorably to the great mystics who submitted their ecstasies to the order of traditional theology. Lawrence did not need this order—(although he was attracted to it between 1913 and 1915)—because he believed that emotion, so long as it remained

5. *Form and Value,* pp. 253–67 passim.
6. Ibid., pp. 263–64.

sincere and vital, would encounter and be checked by its own natural limits. "Up to a certain point, both in mastering, which is power, and in submitting, which is love, the soul *learns* and fulfills itself. Beyond a certain point, it merely collapses from its centrality, and lapses out into the material chain of cause and effect" (P 707). Art would take its cue from life, and there was no need to prescribe the limits of life: to violate them would lead to madness or automatism. Blackmur, distrusting emotion unsupervised by mind and the order of traditional forms, seems to believe that autonomous self-expression will lose itself in infinity, but Lawrence thought differently. In fact, one of his chief arguments against mental consciousness is that infinity only exists as a mental concept. In the blood, "strange gods come forth from the forest into the clearing of my known self and then go back. I must have the courage to let them come and go" (S 26).

Such emotion, when presented in true art, will contain its own opposite. "There is no real truth in ecstasy," Lawrence instructed a fellow writer. "All vital truth contains the memory of all that for which it is not true. Ecstasy achieves itself by virtue of exclusion; and in making any passionate exclusion, one has already put one's right hand in the hand of the lie" (SL 86). In other words, art may, or even should, go to extremes, but "if it be really a work of art, it must contain the essential criticism on the morality to which it adheres" (P 476). The point is illustrated by the West African (or, in a later edition, West Pacific) wood carving that plays an important symbolic role in *Women in Love*. It expresses an extreme of sensual consciousness, but it is genuine art—as Birkin tells us in chapter 7, explaining precisely this point in the Lawrencean aesthetic—because "it conveys a complete truth. It contains the whole truth of that state, whatever you feel about it." The carving is then not simply a symbolic equivalent for a state of being or for any of the characters, as some critics have said. It tells the whole truth about a state of being, and in that sense is more nearly equivalent to the sum of what the novel shows us about one of its characters.

The point is important for a proper understanding of Lawrence's critical procedure. All genuine art by definition expresses and is an expression of vital being. When art leans very far toward one extreme, toward an ideal absolute, Lawrence calls it "almost a lie, almost a blasphemy." But "the artist cannot blaspheme; only the dogmatist can do that" (*P* 476). As he went on, it is true, the critic put more emphasis on the nonvital component and less on its residual life, more on demonic resistance and less on harmonious balance. But however demonic and unbalanced a form it was forced to take, the life principle remained subtle and complex. Neither early nor late did Lawrence, however hysterical his tone and however imperfect his own practice, conceive of art as the expression of hysterical and undisciplined emotion.

·———————————·

Lawrence's theory of form raises some interesting questions concerning the form of his own art, one of which might be usefully considered at this point, if only in a cursory way, to help clarify his position—namely, the difficulties of narrative for a writer more interested in states of being than in social individuals.

Hardy's novels, according to Lawrence, are about coming into being or failing to come into being. When a character achieves a new state of being, "he has become himself, his tale is told. Of anything that is complete, there is no more to tell" (*P* 410). And in his last book, *Apocalypse,* explaining his artistic predilection through an affinitive art, he noted that the images and symbols of primitive man "got nowhere because there was nowhere to get to [;] the desire was to achieve a consummation of a certain state of consciousness, to fulfil a certain state of feeling awareness" (*Apoc.* 77). A conception of narrative along these lines raises a problem which W. H. Auden has succinctly described:

> Like Blake, Lawrence was interested not in "individuals" but in "states." In writing about nature or about strangers this does not matter, as these are only experienced as states of being, but it is a serious drawback in writing fiction which cannot avoid the individual and his relations to other individuals over a stretch of time. Lawrence is never at ease when the time is a long one, so that none of his long novels quite succeeds because we get bored with the lack of a character to bind the states together and give them uniqueness.[7]

There is enough truth in this to explain why Lawrence's short stories, which as a rule describe a single change of state, are usually

7. *The Nation* (April 26, 1947), p. 482.

more successful formally than his novels. Even his short stories tend
to be open-ended and, from a social point of view, inconclusive (a
virtual signature of Lawrencean fiction), but the inconclusiveness is
conveyed by means of ironic juxtaposition, so that there is no loss of
dramatic impact, as there is in the last pages of even his most popular
novels, *Sons and Lovers* and *Lady Chatterley's Lover.* At the end of
"The Horse Dealer's Daughter," for instance, Lawrence plays off the
completeness of the lovers' psychological resurrection against the
groping bewilderment of their social consciousness, with rich ironical
effect. In an equally typical and effective tale, "The Blind Man," a
final consummation in blood friendship between the blind man
Maurice and the mentalized Bertie is ironically revealed on the social
level as a horror to Bertie of which Maurice is unaware.

But the novel is a different case. In his often-quoted letter to
Edward Garnett describing the aesthetic underlying what was to become *The Rainbow* and *Women in Love,* Lawrence warned his mentor
against looking in his new work for a traditional psychology of characterization, and added:

> There is another *ego,* according to whose action the individual
> is unrecognizable, and passes through, as it were, allotropic
> states which it needs a deeper sense than any we've been used to
> exercise, to discover are states of the same radically unchanged
> element. (Like as diamond and coal are the same pure single
> element of carbon. The ordinary novel would trace the history
> of the diamond—but I say, "Diamond, what! This is carbon.
> . . . ") [D]on't look for the development of the novel to
> follow the lines of certain characters: the characters fall into
> the form of some other rhythmic form.   [*L* 198–99]

Auden's criticism and Lawrence's defense of his "other rhythmic form"
are only in a few scenes relevant to *Sons and Lovers* and *Lady Chatterley's Lover,* which are primarily realistic novels; they are very slightly
relevant to the quasi-philosophical novels from *Aaron's Rod* to *The
Plumed Serpent,* whose formal difficulties are mainly traceable to lack
of conceptual unity or lack of conviction.[8] They are obviously most

8. Lack of unity in *Aaron's Rod* and *Kangaroo* is obvious. (But see an
interesting defense of the structure of *Kangaroo* by Leo Gurko in *Modern
Fiction Studies,* 10, No. 4 [1964–65], 349–58.) *The Plumed Serpent* is superficially coherent and has some dramatic tension, deriving from the opposition

relevant to the two major novels, *The Rainbow* and *Women in Love,* and in them I think the artist has to a considerable extent succeeded in overcoming the difficulty that Auden described.

The narrative problem here seems to me roughly comparable to that in *The Faerie Queene,* and Lawrence solves it in a comparable way: by submitting his material to a kind of allegorical scheme by means of which the parts relate to one another not so much causally or consecutively as analogically. In *The Rainbow* this scheme consists of the shifting modalities of relationship in three generations; in *Women in Love* it is the spectrum of vital states between the African-sensual and Nordic-spiritual extremes. The revelation of states of being is presented as a succession of more or less discrete moments of intense relationship: Eliseo Vivas calls them "constitutive symbols," each "a complex situation or scene . . . which gathers the significance of events preceding it and illumines the scenes or situations that follow."[9] The novels grow analogically, as a long poem might, gathering density by accumulating reciprocally reflective moments. This is not to say that there are not traditional and realistic elements in them.[1] But to place them with Jane Austen and George Eliot, as Leavis does, is to ignore the nature and importance of Lawrence's symbolism. Scenes such as the one in which Anna and Will Brangwen gather sheaves in the moonlight or the one in which Birkin watched

---

of the hard actuality of Mexican life to the Quetzalocoatl fantasy and from Kate's sustained resistance to the experience she is undergoing, but Lawrence does not really convince us of his belief in the morality to which the book adheres. Less inventive in creating allotropic states, Lawrence, in these novels, registers the flow of impersonal affectivity by the incantatory repetition of certain favorite adjectives, such as lovely, delicate, suave, sensitive, subtle, soft, unfathomable, mysterious, invisible, dark, splendid, flowing, flaming, warm, hot, vivid, and potent.

9. Vivas, *The Failure and the Triumph of Art,* pp. 277–82.

1. Herbert Lindenberger has argued that the fusion of Romantic and realistic elements is an effective formal principle in Lawrence's long fiction. The fusion is most perfect, he says, in *Women in Love* and in some of the tales, effective but less perfect in "St. Mawr," "The Princess," and "The Captain's Doll" (Moore, *Miscellany,* pp. 377–78). Following this line of thought, one might say that the two streams progressively diverge, the realism attenuating into little satirical sketches like "Things," "Two Blue Birds," "The Last Laugh," the romance becoming fable as in "The Woman Who Rode Away," "The Man Who Loved Islands," "The Man Who Died."

by Ursula tries to break the moon's reflection on the water have symbolic energy far out of proportion to the purpose of furthering the narrative; they absorb us in and of themselves as revelations of states, and Lawrence's prose supports this centripetal interest by rendering in these heightened moments "the actual flow of affective life in relationship . . . the phenomenology of pure experience."[2] The death of Gerald at the end of *Women in Love* does not interest us only or even primarily as an individual and social tragedy, as does the death of Anna Karenina; its interest lies primarily in its symbolic meaning.

Lawrence's theoretical antagonism to traditional form goes very deep indeed, whatever concessions he made to his medium as a practicing artist: "The nearer a conception comes toward finality, the nearer does the dynamic relation out of which this concept has arisen, draw to a close" (*F 108*). "A book lives as long as it is unfathomed" (*Apoc.* 7). "Any thing that *triumphs,* perishes" (*R* 17). For Lawrence any conceptualization, even by means of symbols, becomes a potential prison as soon as it is realized: hence his own critical practice of constantly erecting fresh symbolic categories.

When Lawrence parried criticism of the form of *Sons and Lovers* by saying that "all rules of construction hold good only for novels which are copies of other novels[;] a book which is not a copy of other books has its own construction" (*L* 295), he was doing more than vindicating himself or than protesting against too restricted an idea of form, for no closed, perfected, or already established form could be altogether satisfactory. There is an arresting phrase in another of his angry comments attacking criticism of *Sons and Lovers:* "They want me to have form: that means they want me to have *their* pernicious ossiferous skin-and-grief form, and I won't" (*L* 86). Skin-and grief? It is apparently an allusion to Balzac's *La Peau de Chagrin* (which, Jessie Chambers tells us, Lawrence read with appalled fascination),[3] and, as such, suggestive of his tendency to regard form itself as a prison for the daemon. Closed form seemed to him, in a favorite phrase, a cul-de-sac; the rounded form of tragedy, so often found

2. Vivas, *The Failure and the Triumph*, p. 202.
3. *A Personal Record*, p. 106.

satisfying by others, stood, as we shall see in the next chapter, in particular need of correction.

Behind this profound skepticism lies an even profounder faith. Throughout his career, as Leone Vivante and Joyce Cary have clearly understood, Lawrence adhered with almost monomaniacal constancy to a belief in "the mystery of the inexhaustible and forever unfolding creative spark" (*P* 219).

Vivante gets to the heart of the matter in explaining that for Lawrence "the supreme ontological reality is a principle of unannihilable potency or potentiality." This potentiality is "intrinsically purposive"—i.e. continually seeks for realization or form—but is, at the same time, "perpetually at war with form in so far as formed, and it cannot be reduced to a multiplicity of objective existents." "Thought in its reality as thought"—i.e. as felt by the thinker—"never attains absolute objective determination. Every successive actualization is a new moment of an original potency. . . . This active potency . . . is always new, is always a *primum*. . . . The objective aspect of actualization has no power to annul it."[4]

From his own experience as a practicing novelist, Joyce Cary writes of the artist's simultaneous dependence on the symbol as the only means of realizing his intuition and of his resistance to it because of its tendency to "sink to concept" through formulation and become a crust over fresh intuition. "The symbol, like the concept to which it approximates, is the enemy of intuition. The moment the artist expresses his intuition in formal terms, this expression tends to destroy for him the force of his intuition." The "weakness of the symbol is its failure to be exact either as . . . concept because it carries invariably association of feeling—or consistent as vehicle because it is always sinking back into mere sign." Yet the symbol is all we have to bridge the gap between experience and thought. The "artist who is aware of the crust may invent new symbolic systems." Cary clarifies a point in the Lawrencean aesthetic while explaining his own when he states that, from within, reality appears infinite, though it has actual limits. It is the same point Blake was making when he wrote of cleansing the doors of perception and that the phenomenologist Husserl was making when he wrote of "the inexhaustible infinity of

4. Vivante, *A Philosophy of Potentiality,* pp. 4–9, 79–111.

a priori in our minds"—a phrase singled out for approval by Wallace Stevens.⁵

What Vivante and Cary illuminate in Lawrence—the more so because rage obscures this aspect of his thought—is the idea that creative energy positively *seeks* form and materialization. "The difficulty," Lawrence wrote in an early letter, "is to find exactly the form one's passion. . . . wants to take" (*L* 86). In so often making the appeal from art to life, then, he is not really making the appeal from form to formlessness, from order to chaos. Chaos, to be sure, is often a good word for him: it is the matrix in which man must constantly be renewed; but "the whole goal of the unconscious is incarnation and self-manifestation" (*PU* 16). Norman Mailer, who owes much to Lawrence, phrased the same point for himself when he spoke of "the enormous teleological sense" possessed by the unconscious, "the navigator at the seat of [our] being."⁶

Lawrence's very theology is identifiable with this aesthetic. As Graham Hough puts it, "In Lawrence's thought God only comes into being by actualizing himself in the separate identities of the visible and tangible world."⁷ God cannot think or will things into being:

> But imagine, among the mud and mastodons
> god sighing and yearning with tremendous creative
>   yearning, in the dark green mess
> oh, for some other beauty, some other beauty
> that blossomed at last, red geranium, and mignonette.
>
> [CP 691]

In a phrase: "Religion is the worship of the creative mystery" (*P* 608).

Northrop Frye has called attention to the tendency of civilization "to make the desirable and the moral coincide" and of higher religions "to [limit] their apocalyptic visions to morally acceptable ones."⁸ Lawrence's effort to break the crust over fresh intuition formed by the fixing tendency of ideologies thus leads him to quarrel with civilization itself. The paradox of an ideologue denouncing ideology makes sense when we realize that his own position is, so to speak,

---

5. Joyce Cary, *Art and Reality* (Cambridge, 1958), passim. Husserl is quoted by Wallace Stevens in *Opus Posthumous* (New York, 1957), p. 194.
6. *Advertisements for Myself* (New York, 1959), p. 386.
7. *The Dark Sun,* p. 211.
8. *Anatomy of Criticism* (Princeton, 1957), p. 156.

pre-ideological. "You can't make an idea of the soul" (*P* 611). Again, "Before you can say what art is, you've got to say what man is[, a]nd that, thank heaven, is impossible."[9] Impossible or not, Lawrence was always trying to say what man and, therefore, art is, partly succeeding and then trying again, to recapture the intuition that lives only as potentiality. The priority of life to art is important. If life follows art, it will be following what is already formulated. (Lawrence quotes Wilde's epigram "Life imitates art" with approval, taking both "life" and "art" in a pejorative sense—*P* 752.) If art follows life, it can be made new.

"Questions of form and technique," one of Lawrence's critics writes of him, "were inseparably and probably too simply connected with his attitude to conventions and conventionality in life."[1] The term conventionality is too restrictive. Although some late essays do impugn conventional tastes, the critic considered such a practice demeaning, and in fact he is more than a rebel against conventionality just as he is more than Blackmur's figure of a man who devised an aesthetic to cover up his faults as an artist. Richard Foster has identified the Lawrencean enemy as "the bourgeois spirit."[2] This is a little more useful, but we should remember that he found traces of this spirit everywhere: in Plato, in Shakespeare, in Milton. Indeed, all that we ordinarily understand by civilized morality was implicated. Lawrence quotes Hardy's Jude as saying of Sue, "She was not worth a man's love," and comments irritably, "It was not a question of her worth; it was a question of her being" (*P* 503). With Being as the new moral center, he attempted nothing less than a transvaluation of values. "Truth and Justice are sensual experiences" (*CP* 653); "Honor is an instinct" (*F* 116); "It's not religious to be religious" (*Sons and Lovers,* chap. 9). There is scarcely an ethically charged word of any importance that is not, somewhere or other in his work, transvalued.

The process of transvaluation creates an army of paradoxes. We have the voluntarist denouncing will, the idealist denouncing idealism, the eroticist denouncing love. To some extent, of course, Lawrence

9. From a rejected draft of "Art and Morality," quoted in Tedlock, *Manuscripts,* p. 170.

1. G. D. Klingopulos, from a review of *D. H. Lawrence: Selected Literary Criticism,* in *Essays in Criticism* (July 1957), p. 296.

2. R. Foster, "Criticism as Rage," in Moore, *Miscellany,* pp. 312–25 passim.

simply intends to strip from these words their sentimental increment. But he is not quarreling with the local vicar; he is quarreling with Nietzsche on will, with Plato on idealism, with Jesus on love. At bottom we have a radically individual world view, parallel in many ways to other views but distinctive in itself.

In its prophetic dimension his art as well as his criticism represented a succession of attempts to embody incipient "life" in specific ideals or modes of relationship. But the only ideal that ultimately survived materialization was the ideal of life itself, "the forever unfolding creative spark." Once we perceive this root belief, we can understand more appreciatively the predominance of rage in Lawrence's criticism, for the job of keeping the gateway open was never done.

But if the effort of materialization was, in a sense, self-defeating, it was not futile. Life was inexhaustible and forever new. Moreover, his effort to get behind all conceptualizations, including his own, represented an effort to reimmerse himself in the source of healing. To identify with the creative mystery is to achieve that nakedly ethical relationship to the universe in which consisted true morality and the only true salvation.[3] For there is a true morality anterior to all given moralities. Vivante, Cary, and Mailer make the same point: "The spirit heals . . . because health lies in our deep identity with our own ever-original consciousness" (Vivante). "The individual mind appears to itself cut off from the real except in so far as it can intuit the real" (Cary). "Life is self-affirming; there is no need to speak of good and bad" (Mailer).[4] A nonvitalist like Eliseo Vivas speaks of life as "value-free" and justly criticizes Leavis for using it as a value-term without clearly committing himself to a vitalistic philosophy.[5] But Lawrence would say with Vivante, "Value is a primal reality, absolutely immanent in the act of ordinary perception."[6]

3. Philip Rieff, in his introduction to the Compass edition of Lawrence's books on the unconscious (New York, 1960), says, "Lawrence's personal religion is all going to church and never getting there" (p. xvi). Although this may describe the effect of his thought, it does not describe its intention: "Let them praise desire who will, / but only fulfilment will do" (*CP* 265).
4. Vivante, *Potentiality,* p. 41; Cary, *Art and Reality,* p. 29; Mailer, *Advertisements,* p. 353.
5. Vivas, *The Failure and the Triumph,* pp. 32–33.
6. Vivante, *Potentiality,* p. 49.

With such emphasis on transiency, it may well be asked what kind of permanent value, if any, Lawrence can attribute to art. The question is all the more pressing because we have seen that he identifies life not only with moral value but with aesthetic value as well.

In the course of his essay "Morality and the Novel," Lawrence offers—not intentionally, it seems, but therefore all the more revealingly—definitions of art, morality, and life that are virtually identical, and they will enable us to see how he meets the problem:

> The business of art is to reveal the relation between man and his circumambient universe, at the living moment.
>
> Morality is that delicate, for ever trembling and changing *balance* between me and my circumambient universe, which precedes and accompanies a true relatedness.
>
> If we think about it, we find that our life *consists* in this achieving of a pure relationship between ourselves and the living universe about us. [*P* 527–28]

The common denominator is true relationship between man and his universe. But if true relationship is the report of the living moment, how is art to survive its own day? A metaphysical leap to the fourth dimension solves the problem. The resultant paradox is stated effectively in the same essay:

> When Van Gogh paints sunflowers, he reveals, or achieves, the vivid relation between himself, as a man, and the sunflower as sunflower, at that quick moment of time. His painting does not represent the sunflower itself. . . .
>
> It is a revelation of the perfected relation, at a certain moment between a man and a sunflower. It is neither man-in-the-mirror nor flower-in-the-mirror, neither is it above or below or across anything. It is between everything, in the fourth dimension.
>
> And the perfected relation between man and his circumambient universe is life itself, for mankind. It has the fourth-dimensional quality of eternity and perfection. Yet it is momentaneous.

Man and the sunflower both pass away from the moment, in the process of forming a new relationship. The relation between all things changes form in a subtle stealth of change. Hence art, which reveals or attains to another perfect relationship, will be forever new.

At the same time, that which exists in the non-dimensional space of pure relationship is deathless, lifeless, and eternal. That is, it gives us the *feeling* of being beyond life or death. We say an Assyrian lion or an Egyptian hawk's head "lives." What we really mean is that it is beyond life, and therefore beyond death. It gives us that feeling. And there is something inside us which must also be beyond life and beyond death, since that "feeling" that we get from an Assyrian lion or an Egyptian hawk's head is so infinitely precious to us.   [*P* 527–28]

Art, then, records a true relationship at the living moment, and having done so, achieves a transcendence. It is momentary in that the partners of the relationship are both subject to the flux of time and will necessarily establish a new relationship at another moment of time. But it is eternal ("deathless," "lifeless") in that anything which has achieved complete being escapes time and death.

With his basic naturalism, his resistance to otherworldliness, and his reluctance to find life anywhere but in living things, Lawrence is a little uneasy with the fourth dimension. Skepticism prompts him to imply at times that the absolute itself is subject to cycle, that art does not so much escape time as decay at a slower rate, like Keats's "slow time." For instance, in "The Crown":

This is art, this transferring to a slow flux the form that was attained at the maximum of confluence between the two quick waves. This is art, the revelation of a pure, an absolute relation between two eternities. . . .

. . . it is all the time slowly passing away, unhindered, in its own time.

It passes away, but it is not in any sense lost. Our souls are established upon all the revelations, upon all the timeless achieved relationships.   [*R* 94–95]

Even in the sunflower passage, where the idea of eternity is embraced somewhat more confidently, he is at pains to establish the empirical basis of a life beyond life: "We say an Assyrian lion . . . 'lives.' It gives us that feeling."[7] For complete being is "transcendent but not immaterial" (*R* 211).

Lawrence always endeavors to make the immortality of art follow from the immortality of life. Whatever achieves maximum of being, he sometimes says, even if it is not art (e.g. a poppy in bloom, a cat bristling its fur, a man and woman in maturity), achieves immortality. But one wonders how a dead poppy, for instance, can *outside of art* be "a torch of revelation held out to kindle new revelations" (*R* 215), unless one is to understand a belief in supernaturalism.

It is difficult to identify Lawrence's fourth dimension either with Platonic transcendence or with Jungian archetypes. As one critic put it, "Lawrence tried to specify infinite relationships without recourse to a collective unconscious or a pervasive god and to place the vitality of life in its concrete manifestations."[8] This is a fair description as far as it goes, but his position needs to be defined more dynamically, in terms of his attraction and resistance to each approach. He differs from Plato in rejecting a disembodied spiritual world, insisting on the materiality of being, and emphasizing the Many over the One, but the quest for some single transcendent symbol such as the Holy Ghost or the morning star could not be entirely suppressed. A friend reports that in 1929 Lawrence was still seeking an ultimate symbol: "Sometimes he preferred to call it the central Sun around which all universes revolve and sometimes a great white bird beating water with its wings and sending out waves" (*CB 3,* 297).

7. Not content with that, Lawrence goes on in the following paragraph to show how we go about achieving pure relationships in our daily living:

> This is how I "save my soul," by accomplishing a pure relationship between me and another person, me and the other people, me and the trees or flowers, me and the earth, me and the skies and sun and stars, me and the moon: an infinity of pure relations, big and little, like the stars of the sky: that makes our eternity, for each one of us, me and the timber I am sawing, the lines of force I follow; me and the dough I knead for bread, me and the very motion with which I write, me and the bit of gold that I have got. [*P* 528]

Lawrence's effort to make "life" as concrete a standard of judgment as possible led him to measure not only books but even friends by the degree of life that they possessed—no doubt one of his less endearing traits (See *CB 1,* 73; *3,* 8–9).

8. Mary Freeman, *D. H. Lawrence: A Basic Study of His Ideas* (Gainesville, Fla., 1955), p. 88.

The resemblance between his ideas and Jung's, on the other hand, is sometimes quite close. "Symbols are organic units of consciousness with a life of their own" (P 295–96) is quite Jungian, and Lawrence does not for practical purposes talk of the livingness of past lives or past relationships except insofar as they have become symbols and are thus able to exert a continuing influence on the psyche.[9] To be sure, he locates the fourth dimension not in the unconscious but "between everything." Yet the concept of a collective unconscious is not inconsistent with much of his thought, and I suspect he resisted it because it seemed too static, too abstract (I take "between everything" to be not so much abstraction as evasion), too much a label that tried to settle what couldn't be settled.

What is most alive in a work of art, Lawrence seems to say, is its fluid, dynamic conflict of energies; its resolutions and conclusions only exist to give form and beauty to art, to provide temporary satisfaction through relief of tension; but form is only the outward bound of vital energy, the shell not the egg. It is this more or less Blakean aesthetic, this steady resistance to conceptualization, that makes Lawrence so hard to pin down, so unwilling even to pin himself down, for he rejected outright all descriptive labels, including vitalism (F 62).

In formulating a theory of symbolism, Lawrence is confronted with the difficulty of wanting to express the truth of the imagination as literally and "objectively" as possible without risking abstraction. One

9. There are a number of other striking similarities. Both believed that the spontaneous psychic life is the source of spiritual healing; that this life must be seen from within rather than from without, as Freud saw it; that anything which stirs the psyche is "actual" (Jung) or "living" (Lawrence); that mental consciousness is the cause of spiritual perversion and that a new center of consciousness must be established; that man's present danger is self-absorption and that he must regain his precious naïveté; that primitive man, who did not distinguish between mind and matter (Jung) or objective and subjective (Lawrence), had much to teach modern man in this connection; that, in Jung's phrasing, "the spirit is the living body seen from within, and the body the outer manifestation of the living spirit, the two really being one"; and that (here of course they join Freud and others) the repression of unconscious impulses is fraught with peril.

feels always in his art the *tendency* toward allegory and in his criticism the tendency toward its justification, but he insists that the symbol retain all the subtlety, elusiveness, and suggestiveness that life itself possesses. (Lawrence never called life a principle and disliked calling it a force.) The difficulty of finding a middle ground is evident in his efforts at definition. He firmly rejects allegory because of its explicitness:

> You can't give a great symbol a "meaning," any more than you can give a cat a "meaning." Symbols are organic units of con-sciousness with a life of their own and you can never explain them away, because their value is dynamic, emotional, belong-ing to the sense-consciousness of the body and soul, and not simply mental. An allegorical image has a *meaning*. Mr. Facing-both-ways has a meaning. But I defy you to lay your finger on the full meaning of Janus, who is a symbol.   [P 295]

Again, "we need symbols because a man's blood can't beat in the abstract" (*The Plumed Serpent,* chap 19). But the symbol in some definitions—e.g. "pure percepts of mind and pure terms of spiritual aspiration" (*S* I, 19)—does begin to sound rather abstract. And its application can be rather explicit: the symbol of Moby Dick is praised for its elusiveness, but is finally pinned down as "the deepest blood being of the white race" (*S* 173).

In view of this urge toward the abstract and allegorical, it is not surprising that Lawrence's "symbol" should often slide into "myth":

> It is necessary for us to realize very definitely the difference between allegory and symbol. Allegory is a narrative descrip-tion using, as a rule, images to express certain definite qualities. Each image means something, and is a term in the argument and nearly always for a moral or didactic purpose, for under the narrative of an allegory lies a didactic argument, usually moral. Myth likewise is a descriptive narrative using images. But myth is never an argument, it never has a didactic nor a moral purpose, you can draw no conclusions from it. Myth is an attempt to narrate a whole human experience, of which the purpose is too deep, going too deep in the blood and soul, for mental explanation or description.   [P 295–96]

In *Studies* I, which contains his chief attempt to work out a genealogy of art, Lawrence suggests that art in the modern world is the "fallen" state of myth. And one can discern in his own art an effort to recapture the mythic consciousness. We have noted his tendency to literalize metaphor, to identify the symbol with the experience it is meant to symbolize. The flood that accompanies the sexual union in "The Virgin and the Gypsy," for example, *is* the experience as well as a symbol for it; the two terms of the metaphorical relation are both distinct and identical.[1]

One can see why he was attracted to the pre-Socratic cosmologists. They were trying to construct a kind of vitalistic *science,* to establish, or so Lawrence believed, a middle ground between the Scylla of idealism and the Charybdis of materialism. "In them science and religion were in accord. They gave the true correspondence between the material cosmos and the human soul":

> There certainly does exist a subtle and complex sympathy, correspondence, between the plasm of the human body, which is identical with the primary human psyche, and the material elements outside. . . .
>
> We need to find some terms to express such elemental connections as between the ocean and the human soul. We need to put off our personality, even our individuality, and enter the region of the elements.　　　　　　　　　　　[*S* I, 159–60]

This passage is prefatory to a discussion of Melville, who in his art-speech found such terms.

Struggling toward the formulation of a cosmology that would be felt truth rather than inferred truth, Lawrence speculates boldly. The soul must be unique and underived. "Something is which was not" (*P* 410) is as far as we can go in explaining origins without abstracting from our experience. The scientific hypothesis that life derives from matter and the religious hypothesis that it derives from divine will are both "sheer abstraction." The Dragon and the Serpent are preferable to Jung's libido and Bergson's *élan vital* because they are more concrete (*PU,* passim). Holy Ghost, as we have seen, becomes vital sanity and common sense. Soul is often identified with the column of

---

1. I find suggestive in this connection Vivas' definition of the "constitutive symbol," "a symbol whose referend cannot be fully exhausted by explication, because that to which it refers is symbolized not only *through* it but *in* it. . . . unlike the metaphor where tenor and vehicle are apprehended independently" (*The Failure and the Triumph,* p. 208).

blood or the solar plexus. The business of art, then, is to retain its
moral function without becoming didactic. When Lawrence says that
art provides not just emotional experience but "a mine of practical
truth" (*S* 12), he means a passionate *implicit* truth that "changes the
blood . . . the mind follow[ing] later, in the wake" (*S* 184); the
misleading word "practical" only testifies to his moral earnestness.

Cause-and-effect reasoning is a function of mental consciousness,
useful if kept in its place, which is as a follow-up to intuition. Lawrence's desire to make his intuitions as logical as possible frequently
prompts him to attempt such follow-ups. In *Fantasia*, for example, he
guesses that the suppression of the "upper centres" in modern man
has led to such things as myopia, bad teeth, and tuberculosis. But he
knows that these are inferences. Even in his rather conventional
Movements in European History, designed as a textbook, he is careful
to explain that there is no *cause* for historical movements, that to guess
at causes is only to rationalize spontaneous life-gestures.

It would seem that Lawrence's insistence on identifying the supreme
ontological reality with individual life (in *Fantasia* he explicitly derives
the material cosmos from individual life) is inconsistent with his
belief in the equal reality of otherness, necessary for relationship.
But Lawrence does not worry the solipsistic dilemma philosophically,
as Nietzsche and Sartre do, because, empirically, in blood consciousness,
we are aware both of the reality of our creative identity and of the
reality of otherness: aware of them as primary data. Solipsism is true
only in mental consciousness, "the known self."[2] Mental consciousness

2. William Tiverton (in *Human Existence,* p. 29), reading a passage in
Lawrence too quickly, concludes that he approved of Berkeleyan solipsism.
But the full context reveals an opposite meaning:

> To the known me, everything exists as a term of knowledge. A man
> is what I know he is. England is what I know it to be. I am what I
> know I am. And Bishop Berkeley is absolutely right: things only
> exist in our consciousness. To the known me, nothing exists beyond
> what I know. True, I am always adding to the things I know. But
> this is because, in my opinion, knowledge begets knowledge. Not
> because anything has entered *from the outside*. There *is* no outside.
> There is only more knowledge to be added. . . .
> All this is the adventure of knowing and understanding. But it is
> not the thought-adventure. The thought-adventure starts in the blood,
> not the mind. [*AA* 229–30]

is, like matter, wholly subject to the laws of cause and effect; nothing new and underived can penetrate it. On this basis Lawrence is emboldened to assert that idealism will lead inevitably to materialism (*PU* 12).[3]

One can understand why Lawrence so emphatically defines the value of art in terms of relationship. Only that psychological symbolism which could express subject in its relation to object could intimate an unknown and impersonal rather than a known and personal self, and could thus lead us in an objective rather than a subjective direction. This assumption lies behind his running quarrel with the practice of some Romantic poets, particularly Keats and Wordsworth. In Lawrence's view they experienced otherness too subjectively. He chided Keats for making the nightingale's happy song "a plaintive anthem" and an evocation of death. The song "is Keats, not at all the nightingale . . . [whose song] never was a plaintive anthem—it was Caruso at his jauntiest" (*P* 42, 44). Similarly, he objected to Wordsworth's contemplation of a yellow primrose. Instead of seeing it poised in momentary relationship amid the flux, Wordsworth drew it into the mind. The "something more" that the poet could see but that the yokel (Lawrence's word) could not is only "Wordsworth himself in the mirror." "If the yokel actually got as far as *beholding* a yellow primrose, he got far enough" (*R* 162–70).

The charge of subjectification which Lawrence brings against his Romantic predecessors does not seem very cogent, inasmuch as they were equally concerned with the problem of isolate selfhood and with the imperatives of relationship: perhaps he even explored these subjects less sensitively, for one sometimes detects in his insistence on relationship a violent recoil from narcissism and in his insistence on singleness a violent recoil from merging. Their mode of making

3. The conjunction of the two is illustrated in his satirical story "Things," which presents an idealistic New England couple trying to escape in Europe the materialism of America. The course of their disillusionment is marked by their increasing attachment to "things," until they end up in Cleveland, admiring the vitality of industry. A more subtle illustration is the characterization of the artist Loerke in *Women in Love*. Loerke believes both that "art should interpret industry" and that "a work of art has no relation to anything outside that work of art." Ursula-Lawrence must angrily remind him that his art is only a picture of his own brutality and that "the world of art is only the truth about the real world, that's all—but you are too far gone to see it" (chap. 29).

metaphors was also similar to his: they too not only fused disparities into new identities but also transformed states of the same identity, having cast off the dross of commonplace perception and feeling; Lawrence's sun behind the sun, new heaven, and new earth find numerous parallels in their poetry. What is more distinctive in Lawrence is his reluctance to celebrate the imagination in itself, and his insistence on identifying it with sexuality, resulting in that eloquent but monotonous music which has often been remarked.

Lawrence's blood-mind antithesis itself, as a distinction between spontaneous and mechanical mind, is comparable in static conception to similar distinctions made by Wordsworth and Keats. In dynamic conception, however, Lawrence's psychology entails a more active defensive-offensive against false mind and is closer in this respect to that of a prophetic poet like Blake than to that of a meditative poet like Wordsworth. In his last years, particularly in *Assorted Articles,* Lawrence tends to take a more conventional view of the mind-blood relationship. For instance: "man *can't* live by instinct because he's got a mind. Emotions by themselves become just a nuisance. The mind by itself becomes just a sterile thing. So what's to be done? You've got to marry the pair of them. The emotions that have not the approval and inspiration of the mind are just hysterics" (*AA* 205–06). But I regard such statements as hasty journalism. Lawrence seems to be using the terms mind and emotion neither in the positive nor in the negative sense we find elsewhere in his work, but merely in a popular sense, as if to assure the public that he does not approve of going down on all fours or murdering at will. Essentially, it was not a balance of mind and body that he wanted but a new center of consciousness where mind and body become one. In this quest he belongs directly in the Romantic tradition. And it is worth noting that, despite his basic objections to Romantic poetry (its subjectification of the outer world, especially as it contributes to modern civilization's over-emphasis of the spirit at the expense of the body), he returns to it again and again for his idea of a poem, as he returns to the Old Testament for his idea of a novel.

·┼─────────────────┼·

To round out our view of Lawrence's aesthetic, we must turn finally to his theory of the novel, the subject of several of his most important and interesting essays; however, since Lawrence was not in any strict sense a *genre* critic, we shall find our real subject becoming "art and morality."

All conceptual frameworks, all moralities, err, as we have seen, by denying to some extent the multiplicity and amplitude of life. "Philosophy, religion, science, they are all of them busy nailing down things, to get a stable equilibrium. Religion with its nailed-down One God, who says *Thou shalt, Thou shan't* and hammers home every time; philosophy with its fixed ideas; science with its 'laws': they, all of them, all the time, want to nail us on to some tree or other" (P 534). Because of this, "all morality is of temporary value, useful to its times. . . . Art must give a deeper satisfaction. It must give fair play all around" (P 476).

It seemed to Lawrence that the novel was the form that best gave this satisfaction. It was "the most complex, the most human."[4] It was "the highest form of human expression so far attained" (R 104), "the highest example of subtle inter-relatedness that man has discovered" (P 528).[5] He praised the novel particularly for its ability to undercut given moralities by the very amplitude of its own microcosm, which made possible implicit self-criticism.

> Everything is true in its own time, place, circumstance, and untrue outside of its own place, time, circumstance. If you try to nail anything down, in the novel, either it kills the novel, or the novel gets up and walks away with the nail.   [P 528]

> In life, there is right and wrong, good and bad, all the time. But what is right in one case is wrong in another. And in the novel you see one man becoming a corpse because of his so-called goodness, another going dead because of his so-called wickedness. Right and wrong is an instinct: but an instinct of the whole consciousness in a man, bodily, mental, spiritual at once. And only in the novel are *all* things given full play, or at least, they may be given full play.   [P 538]

4. From a postscript to Verga's *Cavelleria Rusticana* (London, 1928), p. 195.
5. It is interesting to note that Cary also singled out the novel as "the truest revelation of the moral real" (*Art and Reality*, p. 143) and that Mailer found it the most moral of the art forms, because "it's the most immediate, the most overbearing" (*Advertisements*, p. 384).

Let us first deal with the genre problem raised here, before turning to the more fundamental problem of art and morality.

Lawrence uses the word "novel" with varying degrees of license. At times he refers to the Homeric epics, the Bible, Greek and Shakespearean drama, and *The Divine Comedy* as novels. He practically ignores the issue of genre in *Studies,* where he discusses Crèvecoeur, Franklin, Poe, and Whitman, along with Cooper, Hawthorne, Dana, and Melville. His essay "Morality and the Novel" is really about morality and art. In short, he sometimes uses the word as a generic term for literary art or simply for art. Yet he also uses it more strictly, explicitly excluding poetry and poetic drama:

> Being a novelist, I consider myself superior to the saint, the scientist, the philosopher, and the poet, who are all great masters of different bits of man alive, but never get the whole hog. [P 535]
> You can fool pretty nearly every other medium. You can make a poem pietistic, and still it will be a poem. You can write *Hamlet* in drama: if you wrote him in a novel, he'd be half-comic, or a trifle suspicious: a suspicious character, like Dostoievsky's Idiot. Somehow you sweep the ground a bit too clear in the poem or the drama and you let the human Word fly a bit too freely. Now in the novel there's always a tom-cat, a black tom-cat that pounces on the white dove of the Word, if the dove doesn't watch it; and there is a banana-skin to trip on; and you know there is a water closet on the premises. All these things help to keep the balance. [R 106–07]

Lawrence is not exactly pleading here for realism, which, in his opinion, tended to underrepresent life; rather, he is concerned with the perils at the other extreme, the perils of the ideal. Dostoevsky's characters, we remember, were all "fallen angels" whereas "people are only people." Lawrence seems to have felt that the poem, or even the novel tending too far toward allegory, was, by the standards of life—i.e. multiplicity, fullness, concreteness, fluidity—too intense, rigid, abstract, artificial, perfect: in a word, too ideal.

This is not to say that Lawrence did not put a very high value on poetry. In fact, there was something about the very intensity of poetry, the extreme pitch of consciousness which it could convey, that deeply appealed to him. "It is most wonderful in poetry, this sense of conflict contained within a reconciliation" (*P* 478). And he cited a number of Shakespearean and Romantic lyrics as those "lovely" poems "which after all give the ultimate shape to one's life" (*AA* 155). But for the same reason that poetry was most wonderful, it came nearest to losing the real. The poem was less full a microcosm than the novel; the artist's theory of being was less fully exposed to and modified by his living sense of being.

A gently derogatory tone frequently accompanies Lawrence's remarks on poetry, especially metrical poetry. The poems of Keats and Shelley are "lovely" and "gem-like" but not the voice of the immediate present, "artificial," "static," "abstracted from life," "in the storehouse of finished things" (*P* 218–23). Dante is "slightly dishonorable" for worshiping a remote Beatrice while keeping hidden "some vital dark fact," the fact being the poet's "cozy bifurcated wife and kids" (*R* 115) —a judgment, I think, not so much on Dante as on his chosen form, which could hardly accommodate the wife and kids.

Poetry is too formal an art to be discussed effectively without more attention to its formal aspects than Lawrence is willing to give, and it is not surprising that his remarks on poetry are, on the whole, less interesting than those on the novel, a form that more easily yields to an ideological approach. He told Edward Marsh, "Sometimes Whitman is perfect. Remember, skilled verse is dead in fifty years— I am thinking of your admiration of Flecker" (*L* 135). This is hardly convincing proof of the transiency of "skilled verse." There seems to have been something too implacable in the very form of metrical verse to permit the critic to perform with any regularity even his customary partial rescue.

About free verse, on the other hand, Lawrence wrote positively, even rhapsodically, but vaguely. Free verse was the voice of the spontaneous self, "the direct utterance from the instant, whole man . . . the soul and the mind and body surging at once, nothing left out." "Any discord is the discord of reality." "All we can do, deliberately, with free verse . . . is to prune away clichés . . . clichés of rhythm as well as phrase," as Whitman did (*P* 220–21). Good free verse requires "the finest instinct imaginable" (*L* 135) to capture "the hidden *emotional* pattern that makes poetry" (*L* 155). In short, we have some inflated rhetoric, a defense of the fallacy of expressive form, and a touch of insight here and there, usually in reference to Whitman. Lawrence's basic theory of the novel, now including verse treated as if it were a novel (e.g. Whitman's in *Studies*), rests on moral grounds. But it is worked out by way of depth psychology and could hardly be called simplistic. More than the intentional fallacy is implied by the slogans which define his critical approach: "Never trust the artist. Trust the tale" (*S* 13); "Let me hear what the novel says. As for the novelist, he is usually a dribbling liar" (*R* 123). The conscious intentional meaning of a literary work did not, as a rule, interest him. Unless a work appealed to what Vivante calls his "vocation for depth," he preferred to leave it alone.[6] For "unconscious meanings were simply more real, more urgent, more potent, and therefore made the stronger claim; they show what we are, and what we are is often different from what we think we are. It is this, in fact, rather than any special desire to shock or surprise that prompts Lawrence to describe novels such as *Pamela* and *Jane Eyre,* with their latent prurience beneath their manifest amoristic refinement, as more "pornographic" than the ribald tales of Boccaccio (*P* 174).

But the deceptiveness goes deeper. The distinction between novel and novelist is sometimes used to separate manifest from latent meaning and sometimes to separate two kinds of latent meaning, one less apparent than the other. To put it another way, since Lawrence is most interested in how the work reflects the condition of our culture, the dribbling liar rarely refers to bad artistry or imperfectly executed intention; rather, it refers to an intention that reflects an imbalance in the artist's psyche brought about by ideological pressures themselves. And from such pressures the artist, especially the artist of the modern epoch, could hardly be free.

6. Vivante, *Potentiality,* p. 94. Lawrence gives us a clear illustration of his vocation for depth in his essay on Frederick Carter's *The Dragon of the Apocalypse.* After giving a neat synopsis of the Revelation of St. John, he comments: "This is all very fine, but we know it pretty well by now, so it offers no imaginative release to most people. It is the orthodox interpretation of the Apocalypse, and probably it is the true superficial meaning, or the final intentional meaning of the work. But what of it? It is a bore. Of all the stale buns, the New Jerusalem is one of the stalest" (*P* 294). This is not perversity. Lawrence simply means what he says: when a symbolic structure becomes too familiar, it no longer offers imaginative release. He then proceeds to reveal Revelations.

How is this reflected in the novel? How does the novel in the wake of civilized morality become "immoral"?

> Morality in the novel is the trembling instability of the balance. When the novelist puts his thumb in the scale, to pull down the balance to his own predilection, that is immorality.
>
> The modern novel tends to become more and more immoral, as the novelist tends to press his thumb heavier and heavier in the pan: either on the side of love, pure love: or on the side of licentious "freedom."
>
> The novel is not, as a rule, immoral because the novelist has any dominant *idea* or *purpose*. The immorality lies in the novelist's helpless, unconscious predilection. Love is a great emotion. But if you set out to write a novel, and you yourself are in the throes of the great predilection for love, love as the supreme, the only emotion worth living for, then you will write an immoral novel.
>
> Because *no* emotion is supreme, or exclusively worth living for. *All* emotions go to the achieving of a living relationship between a human being and the other human being or creature or thing he becomes purely related to.   [*P* 529]

"Purpose" here is simply that conscious bias which Lawrence spoke of as natural to a writer if he is honest; it can be left to take care of itself if the writer is artist enough to provide the essential criticism on the morality to which he adheres. But "predilection" is unconscious; it reflects the almost inescapable pressures of ideology. What Lawrence is saying is that the urgency that lies behind the novelist's conception of love forces him to one kind of flat simplification or another; that the climate of discussion has made it impossible for the novelist to write about the fullness of human relationships; and that ideas become polarized even in the mind that is not consciously committed to a cause. He concentrates on the predilection for love, taking it to be the greater present danger, but his criticism of either kind of simplification will help us see, as we watch him coming to grips with the modern novel, that he does not himself, unlike some of his cultist critics, advocate "licentious freedom."

> Any novel of importance has a purpose. If only the "purpose" be large enough, and not at outs with the passional inspiration. . . . It is such a bore that nearly all great novelists have a

67

didactic purpose, otherwise a philosophy, directly opposite to their passional inspiration. In their passional inspiration, they are all phallic worshippers. From Balzac to Hardy, it is so. Nay, from Apuleius to E. M. Forster. Yet all of them when it comes to their philosophy, or what they-think-they-are, they are all crucified Jesuses. What a bore! And what a burden for the novel to carry!

. . .

They're all little Jesuses in their own eyes, and their purpose is to prove it. Oh Lord!—*Lord Jim! Sylvestre Bonnard! If Winter Comes! Main Street! Ulysses! Pan!* They are all pathetic or sympathetic little Jesuses *accomplis* or *manqués.* And there is a heroine who is always "pure," usually nowadays on the muck-heap! Like the Green Hatted Woman. She is all the time at the feet of Jesus, though her behavior may be misleading. . . .

Now really, it's time we left *off* insulting the novel any further. If your purpose is to prove your own Jesus qualifications, and the thin stream of your inspiration is "sin," then dry up, for the interest is dead. *Life as it is!* What's the good of pretending that the lives of a set of tuppenny Green Hats and Constant Nymphs is Life-as-it-is, when the novel itself proves that all it amounts to is life as it isn't life, but a sort of everlasting and intricate and boring habit: of Jesus peccant and *Jesusa peccante.*　　　　　　　　　　　　　　　[*R* 104–06, 108–09]

In these keen, outrageous passages from "The Novel" (1925),[7] Lawrence perceives among diverse modern novelists a common predilection for the Christian love-ideal. Among the more sophisticated, it emerges as a preoccupation with sin—a preoccupation urged upon the novel, we know, by writers as different as Eliot and Gide. But immoralism is only the other side of doctrinal goodness; even the hero who breaks from his society retains this ideal in his sense of himself as a sinner. Moreover, the ironic attitude slides easily into cynicism, and the tragic into sentimentalism— which becomes obvious

---

7. "The Novel" was originally titled "The Modern Novel" (Tedlock, *Manuscripts,* p. 173). "Modern" was apparently dropped because Lawrence felt prepared to charge the whole of Western literature with limitation of vision. But he does use the word as a qualifier throughout the essay and does recognize ancient literature as closer to his ideal.

in the less sophisticated modern novel.[8] All of these are too committed to the dominant social ideal to represent "life." "If you are *too personal, too human,* the flicker fades out, leaving you with something awfully lifelike, and as lifeless as most people are" (*R* 110). Like E. M. Forster, such novelists see "people, people and nothing but people," whereas "life is more interesting in its undercurrent than in its obvious" (*L* 605–06).

What Lawrence wanted instead is exemplified by the Old Testament, written "by authors whose purpose was so big, it didn't quarrel with their passionate inspiration. . . . In the great novel, the felt but unknown flame stands behind the characters, and in their words and gestures there is a flicker of the presence" (*R* 110). In the fiction of the more restricted modern era, life seems to be found in two principal forms: first, in the "non-didactic, non-moral" representations of Verga, Hardy, and Tolstoi, once the socially derived increment is stripped away; and second, in such passionate purgations of dead ideals as the classic American novels, buried again under a superficial adherence to the false Christian-Democratic values. The Americans do not fall into the opposite error of advocating licentious freedom, because they would smash the whole goodness-sin complex and establish a new center of consciousness. Whether Lawrence himself managed to escape mere immoralism in some of his fiction is a question, but his theory —less compelled than his fiction to take into account the restraints of actual feelings—is clear on this point.

But even if this narrower purpose is a burden for the novel to carry, an important emphasis in this essay is that the novel can carry it. "All artists are phallic-worshippers" and thus can show us, even through a false, as distinguished from a weak, inspiration, how "one man becomes a corpse because of his so-called goodness, another going dead because of his so-called wickedness." In this sense the novel is an "inherently honorable" form.

This brings us to a statement of the novel's essential qualities.

8. One may be a little startled by Lawrence's association in bad standing of serious and popular fiction. He elsewhere recognizes a difference between the two: the latter has "more illusions about itself" (*P* 527). And he handles the two in a perceptibly different tone: his attack on the popular novel is more relaxed (see "Surgery for the Novel—Or a Bomb"—*P* 523). Still, both present us with "emotions in the old line" (*P* 523).

Fusing the ontological and the ethical in the double verb, Lawrence declares: "The novel inherently is and must be"

1. Quick
2. Interrelated in all its parts, vitally, organically
3. Honorable"   [*R* 116]

The "quick," a favorite word of Lawrence's, is

> God-flame in everything. And the dead is dead. . . . And the
> sum and source of all quickness, we may call God. And the
> sum and tótal of all deadness we may call human.
>   And if one tries to find out, wherein the quickness of the
> quick lies, it is in a certain weird relationship between that
> which is quick and—I don't know; perhaps all the rest of
> things. It seems to consist in an odd sort of fluid, changing,
> grotesque or beautiful relatedness.   [*R* 110]

The assertive and delicate life-flame is not quite an abstraction because it inheres only in phenomena, in creature and setting. It is their inner dynamism, their hidden mystery, the presence in them of "the unfallen Pan." It is also the quality in them capable of acting on the sensuous understanding of man, for the cosmos meant little to Lawrence except in its relation to man. Landscape seemed to him "to be waiting for something to occupy it" (*P* 561). He admired in Melville "the sheer naked sliding of the elements . . . and the human soul experiencing it all" (*S* 158). And he wrote to Frederick Carter, a student of astrology: "If through the Zodiac we can get the human meaning, good. If not, no good" (*CL* 746). We must not be misled by his opposition, in "The Novel," of God and human: by God he means fully human; by human, all too human. If not exactly humanistic, Lawrence's point of view was assuredly anthropocentric.

Thus he especially admired quickness rendered in character. Crèvecoeur had real blood-knowledge but only of snakes and birds (*S* I, 57). Grazia Deledda, a forgotten Sardinian novelist, "deals with something more fundamental than sophisticated feeling," i.e. the Sardinian spirit of place. But "she does not penetrate, as a great genius does, into the very sources of human passion and motive" (*P* 263). Chief among the novelists who *could* render quickness in character were Tolstoi, Hardy, and Verga. Tolstoi "had a marvellous sensuous understanding, and very little clarity of mind" (*P* 479).

Hardy's "feelings, his instinct, his sensuous understanding is, apart from his metaphysic, very great and deep, deeper than that, perhaps, of any other English novelist" (*P* 480). "Verga's people are always people in the purest sense of the word. . . . He had a passion for the most naive, the most unsophisticated manifestation of human nature. . . . Verga turned to the peasants to find, *in individuals* [Lawrence's italics], the vivid spontaneity of sensitive passionate life, non-moral and non-didactic" (*P* 243, 247).[9]

In application, quickness becomes a more concrete touchstone than Lawrence's attempt to define it would indicate: "Vronsky's taking Anna Karenina we must count godly, since it is quick. And that Prince in *Resurrection,* following the convict girl, we must count dead. The convict train is quick and alive. But that would-be-expiatory Prince is as dead as lumber. . . . Pierre . . . in *War and Peace,* is more dull and less quick than Prince André" (*R* 111–12).

As Lawrence proceeds, we see that his second requisite for the novel really overlaps the first. Everything in the novel must be "relative to" or "in quick relation with" everything else in it, and it is because Pierre is insufficiently related that he is insufficiently quick. Lawrence is very specific about this, maybe too specific:

> And this is why Pierre . . . is more dull and less quick than Prince André. Pierre is quite nicely related to ideas, toothpaste, God, people, food, trains, silk-hats, sorrow, diphtheria, stars. But his relation to snow and sunshine, cats, lightning and the phallus, fuchsias and toilet-paper, is sluggish and mussy. He's not quick enough.
>
> The really quick, Tolstoi loved to kill them off or muss them over. Like a true Bolshevist. One can't help feeling Natasha is rather mussy and unfresh married to that Pierre.
>
> Pierre was what we call, "so human." Which means, "so

9. English critics are inclined to emphasize class-consciousness in Lawrence's fiction and to value it for its sympathetic presentation of the affective life of the lower classes. But it seems to me that his basic interest in characterization to a large extent undercuts classes. Certainly he valued Verga's characters more for their "objective" consciousness than for their social submergence. Of course, the two often seemed to go together, but he also found an approximation to what he wanted in Shakespearean and Greek heroes. And in *Women in Love* and elsewhere he himself attempted to render subconscious awarness in sophisticated people.

limited." Men clotting together into social masses in order to
limit their individual liabilities: this is humanity. And this is
Pierre. And this is Tolstoi the philosopher with a very nauseating Christian-brotherhood idea of himself.   [R 112]

So far as one can make sense of this list, it would seem that Pierre is
in quick relation to the spiritual and more overt, material aspects of
life, but not to the sensual or covert aspects, not to anything moving,
gleaming, subtle.

The third requisite for the novel, that of honor, brings us to the
heart of Lawrence's critical approach, for by means of it the critic
measures the difference between what the artist has done with his
materials and what he *might have* done with them. Life is inherent
in real art and in the real artist, by definition. If the artist has been
true to his instinct for life, his art will either reveal the quick or
purge the dead; in either case it will further life. The question is,
then, to what extent has he been true to it.

By the standard of honor, Tolstoi is delinquent in *War and Peace:*

> *War and Peace* I call downright dishonorable, with that fat,
> diluted Pierre for a hero, stuck up as preferable and desirable,
> when everybody knows that he wasn't attractive, even to
> Tolstoi. . . .
> If Tolstoi had looked into the flame of his own belly, he
> would have seen that he didn't really like the fat fuzzy Pierre,
> who was a poor tool, after all. But Tolstoi was a personality
> even more than a character. And a personality is a self-con-
> scious *I am*; being all that is left in us of a once-almighty
> Personal God. So . . . Leo proceeded deliberately to lionize
> that Pierre, who was a domestic sort of house-dog.   [R 116–17]

"It is the thing one most resents in a novel," Lawrence wrote in a
review, "having one's sympathies *forced* by the novelist, towards some
character we should never naturally sympathize with" (P 352). Pierre
might have been quick, or is half-quick, but is finally "mussed over."

It must be emphasized that Lawrence's primary objection is not
the *appearance* of Pierre or any other kind of character in a novel.
"If you put a theosophist into a novel, he or she may cry *avaunt!*
to the heart's content. But a theosophist cannot be a novelist, as a
trumpet cannot be a regimental band. A theosophist, or a Christian,

or a Holy Roller, may be *contained* in a novelist, but a novelist may not put up a fence. The wind bloweth where it listeth" (*R* 120–21). He objects, then, to the novelist's failing to see what the novel itself shows us, that Pierre is not wholly alive. The novelist fails insofar as he projects more sympathy for his characters than we as readers are willing to grant.

We can best see how deep this objection goes in his discussion of *Anna Karenina*, a book whose major characters *are* quick.

> Nobody in the world is anything but delighted when Vronsky gets Anna Karenina. Then what about the sin? Why, when you look at it, all the tragedy comes from Vronsky's and Anna's fear of *society*. The monster was social, not phallic at all. They couldn't live in the pride of their sincere passion, and spit in Mother Grundy's eye. And that, that cowardice, was the real "sin." The novel makes it obvious, and knocks all old Leo's teeth out. [*R* 104–05]

One of Lawrence's critics has pointed out that Tolstoi has attributed to Anna herself a flawed sexual nature, a "corrosive animality," and that she is therefore truly destroyed as much by phallic sin as by fear of society. "Anna may stand for all Lawrence believed in, but I do not think she did so for Tolstoi."[1] Lawrence passes over this because his quarrel is not with Anna for being false to *her* nature, but with Tolstoi for being false to *his*. "Of course Tolstoi, being a great creative artist, was true to his characters. But being a man with a philosophy, he wasn't true to his *own character*" (*R* 116).

In a deeper sense Lawrence is not quarreling with Tolstoi at all—certainly not with Tolstoi the artist, who executed his intention with skill—although the acerbic, personal tone might well lead us to suppose so. He is really attacking that tendency in our culture which caused Tolstoi to go wrong in this way. He attacked Tolstoi because he knew that the only power to combat tendencies lay in individuals.

Lawrence's readers and critics, and I include myself, have understandably been slow to recognize the full extent of his uncompromising assault. Reading the tale against the artist, in the sense of distinguishing between what an artist showed and what he thought he showed, is not an uncommon procedure in criticism. But Lawrence's

1. Constance Smith, *Essays in Criticism* (July 1957), p. 346.

quarrel goes still deeper, beyond formal criticism in any meaningful sense of the term, and becomes ideological. He is not content to lift the disguises from unconscious fears and fixations. He protests against the fears and fixations themselves, against any kind of vital limitation that isn't absolutely natural and inescapable in the human condition. It is clear, then, that if we are to understand him satisfactorily, we must directly confront the ideological basis of his thought.

4

The Quarrel with Tragedy

Lawrence's lifelong quarrel with the tragic as a mode of art and as
an attitude toward life is based on a conception of man's nature as
radically innocent, of his history as a fall from a recoverable glory,
and of his destiny as infinite human possibility. In his heroic effort to
carry so big an idea into an open future, Lawrence constantly ques-
tioned ideas of the inevitable, the necessitated, the determined—in
short, tragic ideas. Examining the great tragic literature of our
civilization, he sought to demonstrate, first, that the dramatist or
novelist, though representing the broadest and deepest civilized consciousness, tends to rationalize, in his tragic conclusion, his—and our
—lack of will; and second, that a more life-enhancing, visionary
significance, present in latent form in the work but unconscious in
the artist, could be rescued from the intended and manifest tragic
meaning. An exposition of Lawrence's quarrel with tragedy will lead
us to an important insight into the nature of his own art, accounting
for qualities in it that have been found repellent by many. Finally,
it may suggest that the imperfect success of his art and criticism is
in large part a consequence of the scope of the task he proposed to
himself.

The error of which virtually every artist in our civilization was
guilty, it seemed to Lawrence, was that of believing that life itself was

wrong, that evil inhered in existence. Assuredly Lawrence was sensitive to evil, even to the point of seeming paranoid. But he gives that impression because he was grappling with "error" at such close quarters. He rejected not only the tragic idea of an existential evil but also the idea of other utopianists, such as Rousseau or Marx, that evil lay in society or in a system of society, and believed that "all malady lies in the heart of man and not in the conditions" (*P* 406).[1] Yet it was only from a still deeper level of the heart of man, his radically innocent core, that evil could be combatted. Man is utterly self-responsible; if we fail to love, "it is our own fault" (*PU* 46). Hence the closeness of rage and reverence, of pessimism and optimism, in Lawrence's work.

Evidently two kinds of consciousness, a true or pure and a false or impure one, are being postulated; let us avoid a plethora of terminology by calling them, as he commonly did, the blood and the mind. The blood, our radical consciousness, is pristine; it contains no bugaboos or devils, nothing corresponding to the Freudian repressed. Lawrence's idea is that the Freudian repressed derives by a secondary process from the mind, implanted in children by parental attitudes and behavior, which themselves derive from the unwholesome ideological climate of civilization. Any determination of instincts is bound to lead to trouble, but especially when the determining ideals have lost their correspondence over the years to some vital movement of the blood and are perpetuated by the mentalized will.[2] All that we call evil—greed and hatred, even selfishness and boredom—are the result of psychic collapse, of the "fall" into self-consciousness. The biblical myth of the Fall is to be interpreted as the fall not into sexual desire but into the sense of sin accompanying desire—which is the true meaning of *The Scarlet Letter* (*S* 94)—the fall not into death but into the fear of death. Not society but "the fear of

1. It is no wonder, then, that he found glib such schemes of perfectibility as Rousseau's or Franklin's, or found intellectualized such phallic worship as Ibsen's, Wilde's, Whitman's or Goethe's.
2. There are really, then, no individual neuroses for Lawrence but only neuroses relative to civilization, only "the general neurosis of mankind," in the phrase of Norman Brown, whose meta-Freudian *Life against Death* works toward the Lawrencean goal of the resurrection of the body through the abolition of repression.

society is the root of all evil" (*CP* 516). And this fear derives "not from within but is poured over the mind, by education" (*P* 392). The trouble begins with the fixing action of the mental consciousness, freezing the fluid impulses of the blood into ideals which then obstruct a fresh flow. If we could get beneath our social consciousness down to the bedrock of our being, and live from there, we would not need either an image of compensatory salvation or an image of ourselves in heroic resistance to defeat: we would not need, that is, either the Christian or the tragic ideal.

This is what might be called Lawrence's ultimate, rather than proximate, view of the human condition. Sex, for example, is ultimately "the great unifier" ("A Propos" 118–19), but in the modern world it is "the great divider" (*P* 197–98), whether it takes the form of demonic destructiveness, as in *The Scarlet Letter,* or the form of egoistic will-to-power which prevents vital interchange, as in Don Juan and Wilhelm Meister. The distinction implies a certain view of history, according to which man is seen has having "fallen" from a state of natural, naïve, religious relationship to the universe into an awareness of himself as cut off from and set against the world around him. As a result of this division, the religious consciousness has degenerated into the social consciousness, the naïve into the tragic, the impersonal into the personal, and the altogether human into the all-too-human.

We can understand more concretely what this entails and what it implies for our subject if we turn to Lawrence's view of literary characterization in the modern era. This view is stated theoretically in that notable letter in which he rejects "the old stable ego of the character" in favor of character pivoted upon a deeper, less determinate center of consciousness:

> that which is physic—non-human, in humanity, is more interesting to me than the old-fashioned human element—which causes one to conceive a character in a certain moral scheme and make him consistent. . . . I don't so much care about what the woman *feels*—in the ordinary usage of that word. That presumes an ego to feel with. I only care about what the woman *is* . . . as a phenomenon (or as representing some greater inhuman will), instead of what she feels according to the human conception. [*L* 197–98]

This is not as simple as it has been made to look, because one is not an exact inversion of the other. The nonhuman character can collapse into human personality by pressure from either of two opposite directions: he may be given too much social consciousness (the fault of a realist like Flaubert) or he may be given too much self-consciousness (the fault of a "higher realist"[3] like Dostoevsky). In the first case he will lack the heroic qualities of depth and splendor; in the second he will lack the open fullness which comes through true relationship to unknown otherness, the religious quality. In either case he will be "commonplace," however extraordinary he seems. This Lawrence explains in two brilliant passages:

> I think it is a final criticism against *Madame Bovary* that people such as Emma Bovary and her husband Charles simply are too insignificant to carry the full weight of Gustave Flaubert's sense of tragedy. Emma and Charles Bovary are a couple of little people. Gustave Flaubert is not a little person. But, because he is a realist and does not believe in "heroes," Flaubert insists on pouring his own deep and bitter tragic consciousness into the little skins of the country doctor and his uneasy wife. The result is a . . . misfit. And to get over the misfit, you have to let in all sorts of seams of pity. Seams of pity, which won't be hidden.
>
> . . .
>
> The realistic-democratic age has dodged the dilemma of having no heroes by having every man his own hero. This is reached by what we call subjective intensity, and in this subjectively-intense every-man-his-own hero business the Russians have carried us to the greatest lengths. The merest scrub of a pick-pocket is so phenomenally aware of his own soul, that we are made to bow down before the imaginary coruscations that go on inside him. . . .
>
> Of course your soul will coruscate, if you think it does. That's why the Russians are so popular. No matter how much of a shabby animal you may be, you can learn from Dostoievsky and Chekhov, etc., how to have the most tender, unique, coruscating soul on earth. And so you may be most vastly important

3. Dostoevsky's own term. Quoted in Ernest Simmons' introduction to *Crime and Punishment* (New York, 1950), p. viii.

to yourself. Which is the private aim of all men. The hero had
it openly. The commonplace person has it inside himself.

[*P* 226, 228–29]

The hero who had a sense of greatness openly is, for example, the
Greek or Shakespearean hero, who had not yet lost his "mysterious
naive assurance" and is "not divided nor cut off. Men may be against
him, the tide of affairs may be rising to sweep him away. But he is
one with the living continuum of the universe" (*P* 541–42). Hamlet
did not succeed in setting anything right in his disjointed world, but
he felt it his responsibility to try, "and so all heroes must feel" (*P* 227).
In short, Lawrence is saying that man is most fully human when he
is part of "some greater inhuman will."

But the tragic mode itself, even in its greatest instances, was
vulnerable to this collapse into pity or self-consciousness:

Tragedy seems to me a loud noise
Louder than is seemly.

Tragedy looks to me like man
In love with his own defeat.
Which is only a sloppy way of being in love with yourself.

I can't very much care about the woes and tragedies
Of Lear and Macbeth and Hamlet and Timon.
They cared so excessively themselves.   [*CP* 508]

This irritable view of Shakespeare is not itself a characteristic emphasis
(Shakespeare's tragedy is more often contrasted favorably to the
smaller-scaled social tragedies of the nineteenth century), but it
points to one. For the thing that irritates Lawrence is inherent in the
nature of tragedy rather than in Shakespeare's handling of it. He
felt that tragedy tended at once to magnify spuriously by creating
pity for the wronged good and to depress by assuming the inevitability
of defeat. It tended, that is, toward sentimentality, and it assumed
that earthly life could not be complete and nontragic.

The assumption underlying such a view of tragedy is one we may
not share, but Lawrence is very keen in pointing to the insidiousness
of the tragic as a habit of mind. Consider his approach to the question
of pity. Not only is the pity we feel for an image of ourselves suspect
morally, since it means embracing our perhaps unnecessary defeat,
but, suggests Lawrence (characteristically joining "ought" to "is"),

79

it may be untrue to our experience as well. In pitying the poor, aren't we perhaps reflecting *self-* pity onto some obvious surface and weeping over our own less than absolute frustrations? May not the pity we feel even for the tragic hero be similar, though on a higher level, and so accommodate us to our fear of being all we could be? According to Lawrence, our instinctive self hates poverty, ugliness, and disease. Therefore true sympathy for the man burdened by them would discriminate between the man and the malady. True sympathy, he says in criticizing Whitman's embrace of a common (Lawrence writes "evil") prostitute or the embrace by Flaubert's St. Julien of a naked leper, would consist of loathing the malady and even the carriers of it insofar as they are attached to it, and of sharing the loathing and desire for cure which they themselves might—i.e. would, in their true selves—feel (*S* 184).[4] However much this lacks in charity, it does call attention to a recognizable aspect of tragic pity. And even if we cannot share Lawrence's faith in the radical innocence of man, as I for one cannot, we might profitably ask ourselves how much of our tragic sense of life rationalizes a lack of will, is really an accommodation to the lesser good.

Lawrence's earnestness is evidenced by the fact that he defined his position against the greatest tragic writers and the ones he most admired. Melville, for example, could be admired for his profound tragic sense because he did not lapse into self-pity, but he was at fault in believing that, because *he* was frustrated, life itself was wrong. Lawrence felt his own plight to be akin to Melville's, but he would not play off "ought" against "is." And so "the world ought to be what it is: a place of fierce discord and intermittent harmonies" (*S* 155–56). Although such a world was less than perfect, Lawrence would neither say that life was wrong nor project an ideal beyond what he felt at any time to be realizable. He was a passionate idealist who was not going to let the ideal lose touch with the real.

.⊢————————————⊣.

Neither tragic art nor its counterpart, Christian art, could give us an image of the whole man, but both sinner and saint could be re-

4. Lawrence discouraged the sympathy extended him by friends during his own frequent illnesses by pointing out that, in illness, there was only half a man left to suffer so that at least part of their sympathy was inappropriate.

garded as following out a vital motion of the soul up to a point. After all, tragedy had the courage to carry the history of the soul into death, and Christianity, at least in its original impetus, into new life, both of which were necessary for achieving "the greater consciousness of the pre-tragic and [the hoped for] post-tragic epochs," the call to which today is "our imperative need" ("A Propos" 115).

It was just because each was valuable in its way that Lawrence was angered by the Dostoevskian mixture of the two, which confused the issue: "These morbidly introspective Russians wallowing in adoration of Jesus, then getting up and spitting in his beard" (*P* 367). The critic penetrates to the source of the confusion:

> Sodom and Madonna-ism are two halves of the same movement, the tick-tack of lust and asceticism, piety and pornography. . . . If there are no saints, there'll be no sinners. . . . If you divide the human psyche into two halves, one half will be white, the other black. It's the division itself which is pernicious. The swing to one extreme causes the swing to the other. . . . But you can't blame the soul for this. All you have to blame is the craven, cretin human intelligence, which is always seeking to get away from its own centre. [*P* 370]

But much worse than Dostoevsky—who was, after all, a great artist and therefore gave us "vital truth," which Lawrence elsewhere reveals—was the degeneration of Sodom into cynical art and of Madonna-ism into sentimental art. These leveled out all feelings as equal. They thus not only failed to lead the soul into new awareness or to destroy the no longer vital but also deadened its capacity to respond to that which could. The tragic was superior to the cynical-sentimental, as Death was superior to Nullity, for "you can make art out of the collapse toward nothing, but you cannot make art out of nothing" (*P* 549).

Tragic art could be especially valuable as revelation of the pernicious tendencies in culture, but to make this possible, the latent visionary meaning had to be rescued from the manifest tragic meaning. The art of Tolstoi and Hardy provided the critic with opportunities.

Anna Karenina is a vital book showing how sexuality becomes destructive in an unbalanced culture. What is unvital in Tolstoi is

Tolstoi-ism, the ideal of Christian brotherhood with which Tolstoi tries to "get beyond his death conclusion"—an aesthetic judgment, by the way, as well as a moral one, based on the perception that Anna and Vronsky are more alive than the carriers of the Christian-brotherhood ideal and on the perception that Tolstoi reverenced the peasants not for their "life," as Verga did, but for their meekness and poverty.

> Let it be a great passion and then death, rather than a false or faked purpose. Tolstoi said "No" to the passion and death conclusion. And then drew into the dreary issue of a false con-clusion. His books were better than his life. Better the woman's goal, sex and death, than some false goal of man's.
>
> Better Anna Karenina and Vronsky a thousand times than Natasha and that porpoise of a Pierre. . . . Better Vronsky's final statement: "As a soldier I am still some good. As a man I am a ruin"—Better that than Tolstoi and Tolstoi-ism and that beastly peasant blouse the old man wore. Better passion and death than any more of these "isms". . . . But still—we *might* live—mightn't we? [*F* 220–21]

Of course, for Lawrence there was a third possibility, which Tolstoi ignored—the possibility of sex as a life-giving force enabling man to be renewed in the larger world, a force that need neither be destructive nor sublimated into an ideal of the spirit. Instead of seeking death or salvation, which are merely different expressions of the same prejudice against the adequacy of earthly life and thus rationalizations of spite or envy, Tolstoi might have been true to his own "column of blood," which, as the visionary critic can see, reverenced the Anna-Vronsky relationship more than the social law that destroyed them.[5]

5. As a youth Lawrence thought *Anna Karenina* "the greatest novel in the world," and Anna the greatest heroine (Chambers, *A Personal Record*, p. 114; also *CB 3*, 593), and toward the end of his life he told his wife's son that Tolstoi's women were greater than Shakespeare's (*CB 3*, 113). He seems to have felt that Anna was that rare thing in the literature of the modern era, a woman of passionate individuality who was neither cruel nor cold.

It is a pity that Lawrence never wrote the book on fictional heroines he once planned (*L* 158), but in a sense the book exists, its pages scattered throughout his work. He found in the fiction of the modern era—particularly the English —as many critics have found after him, the insistent polarization of women into the virgin and the harlot, the good and the beautiful, the light and the

The Quarrel with Tragedy

It would appear that Lawrence is simply not willing to take seriously the social roles of human beings or the claims of society upon men. That is because he believed that the claims of the self were stronger still. But he does not fail to understand society's power, whether exerted from without or from within by our fear-motivated adherence to it. He fights with Tolstoi, or with culture through Tolstoi, for his prejudice against Anna, which is apparent not simply in the fact of her death but in her not being given enough strength to fight society on equal terms. What such strength might consist of Lawrence indicates in an eloquent passage:

> Oedipus, Hamlet, Macbeth set themselves up against, or find themselves set up against, the unfathomed moral forces of nature, and out of this unfathomed force comes their death. Whereas Anna Karenina, Eustacia, Tess, Sue, and Jude find themselves up against the established system of human government and morality, they cannot detach themselves, and are brought down. Their real tragedy is that they are unfaithful to the greater unwritten morality, which would have bidden Anna Karenina be patient and wait until she, by virtue of greater right, could take what she needed from society; would

---

dark. David Copperfield's Agnes is pure and bloodless, his Dora pretty but weak. Pretty Hetty Sorrel must be made flighty. Ardent Maggie Tulliver is to marry a cripple (Chambers, p. 97). (For this, Lawrence revenged himself promptly in his early story "The Daughters of the Vicar," in which the proud daughter says of the "virtuous" but "horrid little abortion" who married her sister: "What right has *that* to be called goodness!"—*T* 60.) Jane Eyre may only acknowledge sexual desire after her Rochester is burned and blinded (*P* 562). Fenimore Cooper, in *Deerslayer,* must gratuitously remind us that his passionate, dark heroine is less worthy than her fair, weak, even feeble-minded sister (*S* 71). Lawrence criticized one artist-friend for denying "the positivity of women" (*L* 75), another for making them "instrumental to the male" (*L* 93). Literature, in fact, presents us with "a long line of Agneses and Gretchens and Turgenieff heroines," of which Sue Bridehead is the revealing end product (*P* 493, 497). Where there are women of both physical and spiritual force (Anna, Hester Prynne, Eustacia Vye, Tess), they are assigned a sense of sin that does not seem essential to their natures. Tolstoi and Hardy are great because they do project sympathy for their "natural aristocrats," but why must Anna and Tess be defeated from within, why must they be attributed a fatal fear of society? Why, in short, couldn't their creators transcend this conflict in their culture?

> have bidden Vronsky detach himself from the system, become
> an individual, creating a new colony of morality with Anna;
> would have bidden Eustacia fight Clym for his own soul, and
> Tess take and claim her Angel, since she had the greater light;
> would have bidden Jude and Sue endure for very honour's sake,
> since one must bide by the best that one has known, and not
> succumb to the lesser good. [*P* 420]

We can see from this that Lawrence's approach to Hardy is similar.
He was fascinated by Hardy's characters for the same reason that
T. S. Eliot was repelled by them:[6] they are so little influenced by
convention (social morality), so much by their own impulses (the
morality of nature). But Hardy, like Tolstoi and unlike the Greeks
and Shakespeare, did not go all the way in penetrating his characters
with a morality of nature. The characters were to some extent
wrestling with mere social convention and were thus "not fully tragic."
Of the three chapters which keep to the subject in Lawrence's long
"Study of Thomas Hardy," the first is devoted to demonstrating
Hardy's default to society; in the last two the critic drops this question
and probes Hardy's art at a deeper level, where it is parallel to the
greatest tragic art.[7]

Hardy contrived his default in several ways. In his early novels
he made his exceptional people villains; thus the community could
punish them and accept the commonplace characters into its fold.
As Hardy progressed, he gradually increased his sympathy for the
"dark villains" (Henchard, Eustacia, Tess, Alec) and withdrew it from
the "white virgins" (Angel Clare, Sue Bridehead). The revenge of
the community was applied rather gratuitously to some of these
(Eustacia, Henchard, Alec): "In primitive times they would have
formed romantic rather than tragic figures" (*P* 438). Even with Tess
and Jude, Hardy shied from fully tragic characterization. He created

6. *After Strange Gods,* pp. 41 ff.
7. This shift in emphasis helps to account for the difficulty in following
Lawrence's line of thinking on Hardy in his brilliant but dense study. The first
of his three close analyses (of *The Return of the Native*) falls in the first half
of the essay, and the second and third (of *Tess* and *Jude*) fall in the second half.
Thus Clym and Eustacia are seen as "sidetracking" their coming into being
by either collapsing into community or being destroyed by it, whereas Tess
and Jude are seen primarily as unbalanced beings, whose tragic end is revelatory
of the state of our cultural psyche.

them, as Tolstoi created Anna, with "a definite weakness . . . a certain inevitable and inconquerable adhesion to community" (*P* 439). They die primarily by their "own lack of strength to bear the isolation and the exposure" (*P* 411). They are thus "pathetic rather than tragic figures. They have not the necessary strength. The question of their unfortunate end is begged from the beginning" (*P* 439).

Now Lawrence shifts his approach. The terms are no longer social morality versus natural morality but the polar forces of natural morality itself: Love versus Law, Male versus Female, Spirit versus Flesh, Christ versus Jehovah. With this new scheme the error of Hardy's art—and it is only Hardy's best art the critic is now concerned with—can be formulated in a new way. The problem is that Hardy unconsciously has a predilection for one side of being (Love, Male, Spirit, Christ) and a corresponding prejudice against the other (Law, Female, Flesh, Jehovah), and thus cannot reflect being as whole and harmonious. He expresses his prejudice by showing Flesh, etc., as either too strong or too weak, destructive or insufficiently fortifying. In Tess it is too passive; in Angel and Sue too weak; in Alec, Arabella, and, to an extent, Jude too coarse and overriding. In no case is Law seen as truly equal to Love.

Because all this seemed to Lawrence evident in the books, he felt justified in correcting Hardy's art to show what he *really* meant. For example, Hardy makes Alec vulgar and Arabella coarse, thus frustrating the fulfillment of Tess and Jude. But "no ordinary man could really have betrayed Tess or drawn from the depths of her being" (*P* 484), and "no ordinary woman would want Jude or could have laid her hands on him," for "Man is as big as his real desires" (*P* 489). Lawrence's ultimate purpose in this essay, as in much of his literary criticism, is, then, not to belittle the artist but to render the deeper meaning of his work. Hardy's "pessimism is a true finding" (*P* 489), as *Anna Karenina* is a "true tragedy" (*F* 220). His novels show us how man "has violated the Law . . . and won death as a reward" (*P* 489).

＊————————————＊

Lawrence maintained his challenge to the tragic idea from the beginning to the end of his career. The only exception was a period after his mother's death (1910–12) when he found the tragic "the most holding, the most vital thing in life."[8] It is the period of his only really tragic novel, *The Trespasser,* which, at that, was reworked from a friend's manuscript. The break occurs in *Sons and Lovers.* Although that novel is tragic in original conception, and although Lawrence continued to regard it as tragic (see *L* 76–78), the revision includes a countertragic or normative pattern of meaning, by which Paul learns from each of his incomplete loves and meaningfully turns from death to life at the end of the book.[9] To the tragic mode proper Lawrence never returned.[1] Concomitant with this challenge was his effort to work out a conception of "true" tragedy, which undergoes at least one considerable change in the course of his development.

The "Study of Thomas Hardy" (1914) contains Lawrence's major early statement on tragedy. There the perspective is so elevated as to be well-nigh Olympian, for at that time Lawrence believed that his rainbow stood on the earth. The vision is of a complete, perfectly achieved civilization, and a place is found for everything. Hardy's Alec and Arabella, whose will-to-power attitude toward love would later exacerbate him, are "good stuff gone wrong" (*P* 487). Sue Bridehead, whose "sex in the head" would set him thundering, must be found a place, as the Greeks found a place for her counterpart Cassandra: "Why should she feel ashamed if she is specialized?" (*P* 510). Even Plato and Jesus, even money and the machine, are fitted into the vast scheme of this work.

The perfect balance, Lawrence tells us near the end, would make the supreme art—identified throughout with the supreme tragedy— but has it been or can it be achieved? It seems to have been most

---

8. Ada Lawrence and Stuart Gelder, *Young Lorenzo* (London, 1932), p. 88.

9. For a good discussion of this pattern, see Mark Spilka, *The Love Ethic of D. H. Lawrence* (Bloomington, Ind., 1956), particularly the chapter "Counterfeit Loves."

1. One might make another exception—and it is an interesting case—of Lawrence's play *David,* written in 1924. It is a kind of parable of the fall of man, showing the supercession of the splendid pagan consciousness (Saul) by the modern ego-consciousness (David). But the play is more complex than this suggests. Lawrence partly favors David for his sensitivity and his capacity for friendship, and, with something like full tragic impact, shows that Saul's loss of power is necessary though regrettable. Significantly, two years later Lawrence wrote to a friend: "If I were doing *David* now, I'd make it more cheerful. Myself I hate miserable endings, now" (quoted in Lawrence and Gelder, p. 148).

nearly achieved by Aeschylus, who, "having caught the oriental idea of Love, correcting the tremendous Greek conception of the Law with this new idea, produces the intoxicating satisfaction of the Oresteian trilogy. The Law, and Love, they are here the Two-in-One in all their magnificence" (P 476). Yet Lawrence is so loftily visionary and at the same time so distrustful of the already achieved that even Aeschylus' art finally falls a little short: "he still adheres to the Law. . . . What he has learned of Love, he does not yet quite believe" (P 482).[2]

What Lawrence is after in this essay, and the standard by which he finds all tragedy wanting, cannot itself reasonably be called tragedy at all. His search for an art which impassively presents the total complexity of inevitably opposed yet valid claims is reminiscent of Hegel. Yet in his resistance to investing either claim with the intransigent completeness that produces a tragic dilemma, he is nearer to Blake. Like Blake, he seems to regard the contraries as a division within man which may be elevated to a seeming conflict of absolutes, but which collapses into unity once any such absolutism is discredited. His equivocation with regard to Aeschylus (and we find it again with regard to the Old Testament in "The Novel," where the conception of God is almost perfect but just a little too intimate and personal) is the product of a desire to find a perfection within history combined with an almost-as-strong reluctance to find perfection anywhere but in possibility itself.

Both the utopian impulse and the impulse to regard art and life as coterminous are profoundly and characteristically Romantic, and the conception of art which they lead to should probably be called apocalyptic or visionary rather than tragic. Its dynamic is the revela-

2. I quote only the conclusion of a rich, compact discussion of Aeschylean tragedy, P 481–82. Richard Foster is not correct in stating that Lawrence "seconded the greatness that tradition had conferred upon Shakespeare, Homer, and the Greek tragedians, but he wrote nothing about them" (Moore, *Miscellany*, p. 314). On Shakespeare, as a matter of fact, he commented more often than on any other writer, as my appendix will show, and the ten-page discussion of *Hamlet* in *Twilight in Italy*, part of which is quoted in Chapter 5 of this study, is of very great interest and value. On Homer and Sophocles he also made some interesting remarks. See the appendix for a complete list of references.

tion of the ongoing about-to-be rather than the working out of established laws. The visionary artist is deliberately naïve in order not to inhibit his inspiration, but his work is not finally without the complexity of irony, arising from the discrepancy between vision and actuality. But the more common irony of the tragi-comic mode, which arises from the discrepancy between actuality and established ideal, is not needed or wanted.

The conclusion of "Thomas Hardy" is both visionary and skeptical. Lawrence tells us that "the supreme art remains to be done" (*P* 516), but he implies that it cannot be done until life itself becomes perfect.[3] One can hardly resist the conjecture—so much does the essay read like a complex blueprint for *The Rainbow*—that Lawrence was challenging himself to the achievement of that supreme art. Yet one senses at the end of that novel his retreat from an ideality which he felt life itself had not yet attained. His doubt was to become stronger, but his visionary intensity remained, prompting and outliving a succession of embodiments.

---

3. In a letter of 1915, commenting on Van Gogh's tragic awareness of the dichotomy between art and life, Lawrence expresses his belief in the ultimate unity of the two. The passage is worth quoting also to demonstrate that the Lawrencean ideal, for all its metaphysical elaboration, is fundamentally a social conception:

> I see Van Gogh so sadly. If he could only have set the angel of himself clear in relation to the animal of himself, clear and distinct but always truly related, in harmony and union, he need not have cut off his ear and gone mad. But he said, do you remember—about "in the midst of an artistic life the yearning for the real life remains" —*"one offers no resistance, neither does one resign oneself"*—he means to the yearning to procreate oneself "with other horses, also free." This is why he went mad. He should either have resigned himself and lived his animal "other horses"—and have seen *if his art would come out of that*—or he should have resisted, like Fra Angelico. But best of all, if he could have known a great humanity, where to live one's animal would be to create oneself, *in fact, be the artist creating a man in living fact* (not like Christ, as he wrongly said)— and where the art was the final expression of the created animal or man—not the be-all and being of man—but the end, the climax. And some men would end in artistic utterance, and some wouldn't. But each one would create the work of art, the living man, achieve that piece of supreme art, a man's life.   [*L* 233]

After *The Rainbow* (1915) Lawrence's thinking takes a sharp turn. It is marked by a shift from a basically Christian, static, metaphysical structure (the Father and the Son as complementary antinomies reconciled by the Holy Ghost) to a basically pre-Socratic, dynamic structure (destruction and creation, death and rebirth). The quest is no longer for a supreme balance of opposites but for the supercession of a finished mode of being. The old must be destroyed before the new can appear. Lawrence introduces in "The Crown" (1915) the concept of vital death or creative destruction. He thinks now in terms of heroes of death (such as Attila, destroyers of the no-longer vital, who permit rebirth to occur) and heroes of rebirth (such as St. Paul, preservers of the newly vital after a time of creative crisis). He now believes that "every new conquest of life means a 'harrowing of Hell' " (*Apoc.* 114) and that only "when we understand our extreme being in death [have we] surpassed into new being" (*P* 676).

The major forms of obstructive ideals were the Christian ethic and its modern offspring, the democratic ethic—i.e. materialism, the mere inversion of idealism. In "Thomas Hardy" Lawrence had come not to destroy but to fulfill the law, to add the resurrection to the crucifixion, as at the beginning of the Christian era. But a year or two later he came to believe that the predilection for Christian love had gone so far as to necessitate a creative destruction. The crucifixion was no longer, to use Blakean terms, a Contrary but a Negation. In his prefatory manifesto to "The Crown" he declared: "It's no use trying merely to modify present forms. The whole great form of our era will have to go." He could not fall back on a belief in cyclical history and an eternal return although his thought continued to verge on the idea, because return might no longer be possible beyond a certain point.

There are, then, two kinds of death for Lawrence: the vital death necessary for progression, the contrary; and nullity (evil, the spirit of mechanical antilife), the negation. The first is life-enhancing, because it "promotes the flow"; the other is life-denying, because it "impairs the flow" (*R* 130). Evil is "the third thing," after life and death (*CP* 710–11). "Death is not evil, evil is mechanical" (*CP* 713).

For the most part, Lawrence, like Blake, conceives of the Dantesque or Miltonic hell as the half-part of life. "Satan only fell to keep a balance" (*CP* 710). But his hell and heaven lack the Blakean equipoise. One reason for this is that, feeling that heaven had become a nullity, he tended to associate hell with the whole life of the body.[4] A second reason is that Lawrence was a little less willing than Blake to think of history as a purely individual affair, a little more inclined to think of revolution in terms of society. In these respects Lawrence's hell seems nearer Shaw's than Blake's. For Shaw, too, hell represented, in vitalistic and non-Christian terms, the evil of outlived social ideals.

Although Lawrence identified evil with mechanical nonbeing, it is important to understand that he regarded it as active and powerful. "The soul is a very perfect judge of her own motions, if your mind doesn't dictate to her" (*S* 189)—but the mind *does* dictate. And its dead ideals, working down from mental to blood consciousness, "motivising affective centres by means of ideas mentally derived" (*PU* 29), could goad "life" into demonic revenge. Particularly during his so-called power period (1920–25), he believed that vital being had become so oppressed that it must assume a demonic role as a nemesis to an evil civilization. Sometimes he saw modern woman, unfulfilled because of modern man's loss of power to lead, as the vehicle for this nemesis. Such is the meaning he assigned during this period to Hester Prynne, Anna Karenina, and Sue Bridehead; their effect on Dimmesdale, Vronsky, and Jude was destructive, because the polarity between man and woman had broken down (*P* 197, *F* 218–20, *S* 99–110). In his own fiction the demonic is usually represented by alienated being made savage in resistance to the ubiquitous evil—e.g. the young man in "The Fox," St. Mawr, and Romero in "The Princess." Lawrence did not idealize the demonic. If it had a kind of beauty, it also had a kind of repulsiveness, because it had been denied natural fulfillment. But even more emphatically, he did not consider the demonic "evil." As Kingsley Widmer points out in an excellent discussion of the problem: "In Lawrence's dialectic, this positive evil can only be overcome by the demonic denial. With a subtlety characteristic of romantic thought, and antithetical to more dominant moralities and religions, evil and the demonic are not equated, and indeed become the ultimate choices."[5]

4. Frederick Carter, in his undervalued little book *D. H. Lawrence and the Body Mystical* (London, 1932), reports that Lawrence spoke of putting Satan outside the Christian scheme altogether, that he wanted to make him the hero of a paradise regained, a pre-Adamic hero come to restore the lost life of the body (pp. 29 ff.).

5. In Moore, *Miscellany*, p. 21.

Demonic destruction is morally justifiable to the revolutionary vitalist because "pure passionate destructive activity and pure passionate constructive activity are the same, religiously" (*F* 124); underlying it is his profound faith that new life will emerge from cataclysm. A rationalist like Freud, who also pondered the toll which civilization takes on our instinctual life, permitted himself to hope only that Eros might rouse itself to equal power with Thanatos. But Lawrence dared even to welcome cataclysm in the faith that "nothing will ever quench the human potentiality to evolve something magnificent out of a renewed chaos" (*F* 55).[6]

Clearly for Lawrence there is a death to be died, and on that basis he revised his concept of a "true" tragedy. Its paradigm is the Book of Job, which gives us the death of *egotism* rather than the death of the *sinner* (*SL* 186–87). Job properly begins at the point where Hardy's Jude ends: cursing the day of his birth (*P* 481). Physical death is not the important issue, for "death doesn't matter once we *are*" (*R* 95). In fact, Lawrence seems to prefer that the artist avoid it in order to point up the true issue, which is vital death, "a climax in the progression towards new being."[7]

The novels between *Women in Love* (1916) and *The Plumed Serpent* (1925) contain, accordingly, the dual rhythm of repudiation and promise—the substance of that promise being, to risk oversimplification, man to man love as a complement to marriage in *Women in Love;* leader and follower friendship as a modification of man to man love in *Aaron's Rod;* "pure isolate integrity" in *Kangaroo* and *The Boy in the Bush.* But Lawrence's fanatic adherence to the truth of the living moment makes him reject the substance of each promise almost as quickly as it is conceived. Even *The Plumed Serpent,* which orchestrates all these motifs and which he called in 1925 "my most important novel so far" (*L* 637), is soon afterward rejected (*L* 711).

After 1925 Lawrence's sense of promise, like his health, becomes noticeably more frail. Demonism attenuates into satire, as in "Mother and Daughter," "The Blue Moccasins," and "Things." Apocalypse

6. Cf. Mailer: "The affirmation implicit in the proposal that all moral restraints be removed is that man would then prove to be more creative than murderous and so would not destroy himself" (*Advertisements,* p. 354).

7. *Touch and Go* (New York, 1920), p. 11.

softens into idyll, as in "The Man Who Died," "The Virgin and the Gypsy," and *Lady Chatterley's Lover.* The search for a better world is more discursive, relaxed, and remote, less dramatic, urgent, and immediate, as we can see in *Etruscan Places,* "Introduction to These Paintings," "A Propos of Lady Chatterley's Lover," and *Apocalypse.* But the visionary passion remains. It is sometimes rather stark, as in the opening line of his last novel—"Ours is a tragic age, so we refuse to take it tragically"—or as in the poignant little poem:

> Desire may be dead
> And still a man may be
> A meeting place for sun and rain
> Wonder outwaiting pain
> As in a wintry tree.   [*CP* 504]

And sometimes it recaptures, as in the fine *Last Poems,* where the imminence of death stirred Lawrence's imagination, a vivid splendor. But there is no fundamental recantation.

The sympathy for the Catholic Church expressed in "A Propos of Lady Chatterley's Lover" is not really a new acceptance of Christianity; it is rather an extension of Lawrence's argument against the Protestant-democratic-scientific emphasis on universal self-realization and a demythicized cosmos. It goes along with his new sympathy for Dostoevsky's Grand Inquisitor, whose objections to Christ's unreasonable demands on the ordinary man are now seen as unanswerable. Lawrence has returned, by a circuitous route and in a more wistful manner, to the grand social conception of *The Rainbow* period. He now understands that "when you teach people individual self-realization who are only capable of fragmentariness, you only make them envious and spiteful," and that "anyone who is kind to man wants to arrange a society of power in which man naturally falls into a collective wholeness" (*Apoc.* 168, 170). Some conception of this sort the Church has been able to preserve.

⊶————————————⊷

Throughout, Lawrence expressed his vision in modes of art that fall along an axis we may call, to use Northrop Frye's terminology, the apocalyptic-demonic, and resisted the modal axis, which may be called the tragi-comic.[8]

It seems to me much more profitable to talk of the moral implications of Lawrence's vision in terms of the mode that carries it than to talk of them—as so many critics, hostile and friendly, have done—as social questions. The "insensibility to ordinary social morality," which T. S. Eliot found in Lawrence, and which almost every critic since has condemned or justified from a social point of view, can be understood as an inherent feature of his mode. For the apocalyptic-demonic, in order to be fully human according to its own understanding of the human, cannot be fully human in the tragi-comic sense. Its purpose is to carry out, so far as imagination and felt belief permit, a radically individual vision of being. It must stop short of social consequences. The social exclusion or inclusion, integration or reintegration, which is characteristic of the tragi-comic mode, is not its business.

If we are going to take Lawrence seriously as an artist, we must grant him his mode. It may be objected—and rightly—that he did not grant other artists theirs. But he is criticizing them from a definite position. He is giving the essential criticism of one mode on the other. The argument may, of course, be reversed, but this is seldom done. Instead, Lawrence's critics criticize his deficient moral sense or deficient humanity. Consequently, lacking a definite position, their moral criticism becomes what his moral criticism does not become: irrelevant. Ignorant of his mode, they fail to draw the really proper inference from their resistance to his art: that they don't like *that kind* of art.[9]

Let me take a simple example of this confrontation of modes, which may clarify these remarks and extend their applicability. I am thinking of Rousseau's well-known comment on the sincerity of Molière's misanthrope: the dramatist was ridiculing what he should

8. Hough, in *The Dark Sun* (p. 257), uses the word "idyllic" to describe the anti-tragic Lawrencean mode—which is perhaps too mild. The word Lawrence himself opposed to "tragic" was "rhapsodic" (P 58).

9. T. S. Eliot to some extent confronts Lawrence the way Lawrence confronts other artists, but insofar as Eliot pretends to be giving us disinterested judgment rather than judgment from a point of view, his criticism is less honest than Lawrence's.

have praised. If, say, an undergraduate were to make this comment, we might be tempted to discourse upon the affective fallacy; perhaps we should tell him that he missed the point. Actually, his comment would be to the point, but not very interesting. It becomes interesting from Rousseau, I believe, because of the force, the complexity, and the intrinsic interest of the vision that informs it.

A curious and perhaps disturbing feature of apocalypse is its lack of humility. It seeks to impose itself as the whole truth, the only truth. Clifford Chatterley, for example, would be no crueler a characterization than Shakespeare's Malvolio or Molière's Harpagon if he were done in the comic mode. But the idyll of Mellors and Connie is the only truth, and there is no room for Clifford: he cannot be laughed at; he cannot be forgiven; he must be repudiated.

Yet why does this disturb us more in Lawrence than in other writers of a comparable tradition, such as Blake and Shelley? It cannot only be that Lawrence is nearer to us. Surely it is also because he carries his banner right into the enemy camp: he writes novels—that is to say, he creates social situations and refuses social consequences. Why do Ibsen and Shaw seem less terrifying? They, too, were iconoclasts who shared Lawrence's hatred of outlived ideals and embraced in their ways something like his faith in life. My guess would be that their respective use of tragedy and comedy softened the force, not of their art, but of their assault on the reader. Despite the strength of their social criticism, Ibsen and Shaw were led by their very mode to work out the consequences of their vision in social terms and thus to divide the responsibility for change between the individual and society. They did not put the responsibility, as Lawrence did, and as his mode required, entirely upon the individual.[1] Nietzsche and Yeats, in many ways heroic vitalists like Lawrence, might also be contrasted to him in this respect. Favoring the stately and noble, both admired the definite, rounded form of tragedy.[2] Both were also able to adopt a

1. Ibsen and Shaw both, it is interesting to recall, moved nearer the apocalyptic mode in their late work.
2. Compare Yeats' advocacy of the metrically regular short poem that "clicks shut like a box" to Lawrence's advocacy of Whitmanesque free verse, which, unlike the "gem-like lyrics of Keats and Shelley," is able to capture "the pulse of the living moment." More strikingly, compare their interpretations of the theosophical symbol, the serpent with the tail in its mouth: to

cyclical view of history without too much skeptical undercutting and could thus meditate more impassively than Lawrence permitted himself to do on the course of human endeavor.

One might venture to assert, then, that of visionary thinkers of the modern epoch Lawrence is at once the most earnest and the most skeptical, the one most intent upon identifying vision and fact, art and life, the infinitely possible and the stubbornly actual. Reverencing one, he sometimes strikes us as an enemy of the other; reverencing both together, he seems to be trying the impossible.[3] He wants myth but he wants history. He exalts Blakean Mind but also Rousseauistic Nature. He remained a divided man in a divided age, heroically determined to make himself and it whole. The sheer size of his ambition must be a major reason for the comparative unsteadiness and inconsistency of his art and thought.

Yeats this represented unity of being, the harmony of the upper and lower selves; to Lawrence it represented spiritual imprisonment, the ego turning round and round upon itself.

3. A striking feature of Lawrence's art which illustrates this unstable tension is its yearning to break from the limits of naturalism altogether and yet its reluctance to do so. Given his temperament—propulsively exploratory, tempted by extremes—it is not surprising that his tales do occasionally break naturalistic bounds and become "ghost" stories: e.g. "The Borderline," "The Rocking-Horse Winner," "The Last Laugh," and "Glad Ghosts" (it is pertinent to note that in theme, however, these stories are *critical* of supernaturalism). More characteristic is a tale like "The Man Who Died," in which Lawrence is evidently tempted to present the crucifixion and hence the resurrection as total, but must make it clear that he is speaking of a man who *almost* died.

There is a curious piece in *Phoenix* called "Autobiographical Fragment," which begins quite naturally as an account of the author's return to the Midlands and suddenly becomes a fantasy in which the time is 2027 A.D. and the first-person narrator has awakened into a kind of unfallen world. Lawrence carries the fantasy forward rather weakly for a page or two and then drops it. One gets the impression that he felt driven beyond naturalism, and in very personal terms, by the intensity of his wish, and then lost his creative drive in that rarefied air.

5

Myth and History

Theories [of Western cultural tradition] fall into two main groups, the going-up and the going-down. The going-up one started as the humanistic view, predominant from the sixteenth to the eighteenth century and implied in the title of Gibbon's *Decline and Fall*. This is a U-shaped parabola reaching its bottom with "the triumph of barbarism and religion" in the Dark Ages and moving upward with the revival of learning. . . . The complementary or Romantic view is an inverted U rising to its height in medieval "Gothic" and falling off with the Renaissance, and is most articulate in Ruskin.

In the late nineteenth century the going-up parabola lost its opening curve and developed into a theory of progress. . . . The descendant of the Ruskinian view we may call, in an image of *The Waste Land,* the bobsled or "down we went" theory. According to this, the height of civilisation was reached in the Middle Ages, when society, religion, and the arts expressed a common set of standards and values. This does not mean that living conditions were better then . . . but that the cultural synthesis of the Middle Ages symbolises an ideal European community. All history since represents a degeneration of this ideal.[1]

1. Northrop Frye, *T. S. Eliot* (New York, 1963), pp. 7–8.

The Romantic view of historical degeneration, deftly summarized by Northrop Frye, achieved a remarkable apotheosis among English and American belletrists in the early years of this century. Within a dozen years (1905–17) writers as diverse as Henry Adams, T. S. Eliot, Ezra Pound, T. E. Hulme, Wyndham Lewis, W. B. Yeats, and D. H. Lawrence independently worked out theories of an historical Fall—i.e. adapted the Judeo-Christian myth of the Fall to an historical frame of reference. The effort represented perhaps a third phase of post-Romantic sensibility, recapitulated in the career of Yeats: first, nostalgia for a more beautiful past, prominent in Victorian literature; second, repudiation of an ugly present, prominent in late Victorian literature and remaining as a salient feature in the work of these writers; and third, a prophetic orientation to the future, in some cases covert. These writers attempted to discover "some kind of disastrous psychical shift, some original moral catastrophe in human history, about the time of the Renaissance, and to couple this with the belief that another crisis, another major alteration of sensibility was at hand."

The quotation is from Frank Kermode, who has studied this phenomenon—mainly in connection with Yeats, and to some extent with Eliot, Hulme, and Pound—in his book *Romantic Image*.[2] Kermode offers two explanations. The first, which helps to account for the mythmaking impulse, is that a belief in an historical Fall was forced on these writers by their aesthetic belief in "some reality imperceptible to the senses and without phenomenal equivalent."[3] From here it is

2. Frank Kermode, *Romantic Image* (New York, 1957), p. 124 and passim.
3. Ibid., p. 111. Kermode's concept of the Romantic aesthetic as a belief in a supernal order of reality is illustrated in Lawrence by such terms as "pure relation," "eternity," and "the fourth dimension." The quotation from Gérard de Nerval which Kermode cites as characteristic of this aesthetic—"poetry should be a miracle, not a hymn to beauty, nor a description of beauty, nor beauty's mirror, but beauty itself"—closely approximates, in phrasing as well as meaning, Lawrence's reflections on the fourth-dimensional qualities of Van Gogh's sunflowers, quoted on p. 54. The devaluation of intellect, of rhetoric and discourse (debased in the market place), and of all merely intellectual uses of language, which Kermode observes in various Romantic theorists, is obvious in Lawrence. Intellect is to be expelled from the House of Being—though, chastened and humbled, it may sometimes be readmitted at the back door. Science and philosophy are not alternative means of seeking knowledge but are inferior to the true way of art-speech. And one can detect

but a step to some such concept as Yeats' Great Memory, the store-house of archetypal images, the timeless and self-contained universe of myth.[4] The second, which helps to account for the fact that the mythmaking impulse was turned upon history, is that a belief in a better past age—and in an imminent return to something like it—helped these writers to come to terms with a present world that offended them socially and imaginatively, a world from which they felt, as artists, more and more estranged; for, finding no outlet in action, they were driven into greater self-consciousness, which in turn cut them off still more from society.[5]

Let me try to clarify their dilemma by putting the matter another way. As heirs to the tradition of modern science, they could no longer use myths as "naïvely" as Milton could. Yet as heirs to the Romantic tradition, they felt impelled to quest for an order of reality which could offer social and metaphysical support comparable to that of the old myths. The response of the original Romantics had been, of course, to make from the tension between aspiration and actuality an

----

in Lawrence, as in the others, evidence of resentment against the very necessity of language—for example, "There was always confusion in speech, yet it must be spoken" (*Women in Love*, chap. 19); tacitly, he also assented to the Romantic belief that art aspires to the condition of music.

4. Lawrence was apparently too skeptical of stability, permanence, and abstraction to adopt openly some such concept as Yeats' Great Memory, Joyce's stasis, or Jung's collective unconscious, a concept that Kermode takes to be necessary to this aesthetic, but something of the sort is implied in "an infinity of pure relations" (*P* 528) or in "Our souls are established upon all the revelations, upon all the timeless achieved relationships" (*R* 94). See the discussion above, pp. 54–57.

5. This is brought out poignantly in Lawrence's early novel *The Trespasser*, especially pages 76 and 180. In later work Lawrence eschews any attitude that borders on self-pity, but his sense of alienation as an artist is frequently implied in his reactions to his reading about other artists:

> I'm reading Beethoven's letters—always in love with somebody when he wasn't really, and wanting contacts when he didn't really—part of the crucifixion into isolate individuality—*poveri noi*.   [*L* 694]

> I am reading the Dostoievsky letters. What an amazing person he was—a pure introvert, a purely disintegrating will. . . . But he is a great man and I have the greatest admiration for him. I even feel a sort of subterranean love for him. But he never wanted anybody to love him, to come close to him.   [*SL* 108]

individual myth, to draw from their own imaginations the needed support, to resist their age, making themselves scapegoat-heroes in doing so.

And this was the response of their truest descendants among the writers under consideration, Lawrence and Yeats. Yearning for an age in which the artist was one with his audience and the mind one with the body, they formulated myths of the redeemed self and the redeemed society, in which the pairs were again united. They bitterly but courageously accepted the fact that creative activity had to be an individual rather than a collective effort. And they were willing to suffer representative destinies, to make their lives public allegories of human aspiration.

•————————————•

"At its worst," observes Kermode, "[the historical myth created by these writers] is merely a way of saying which facts one likes[;] at its best, it is an interesting primitivism, looking for an unmodern virtue not in a remote past but in Christian Europe."[6] It would be difficult to claim much more than this for the practice, although one should not omit to mention the many perceptive value-judgments on details and phases of cultural history which the best of them, combining a sensitive aesthetic awareness with their strong moral biases, are able to make within their schemes. Lawrence's myth, moreover, is less coherent than Yeats' and less plausible than Eliot's, but it is, I believe, peculiarly interesting for what might be called its very defects. To an extraordinary degree Lawrence was willing to give himself away, which means that he more fully explored the grounds and limits of this idea than did Eliot, whose restraint obscured his tendentiousness, and Yeats, whose credulity submerged his own doubts. Not the most notable aspect of Lawrence's literary criticism, it is nevertheless interesting enough to be worth a chapter's discussion.

Lawrence first developed his view of an historical Fall (it is almost exclusively *cultural* history that interests him and the others) in two lesser known works: *Twilight in Italy* (written 1913, published 1916) and "Study of Thomas Hardy" (written 1914, published posthumously). It was modified and elaborated in random comments thereafter;

6. *Romantic Image*, p. 146.

and in some of his later essays, chiefly "Introduction to These Paintings" (1929), it was, in revised form, fully restated. With these works
as foci we can sketch in the theory fully enough. The next few pages,
then, will be primarily discursive, and the implications of the theory
will be examined afterward.

Commenting on *Hamlet* in an essay called "The Theatre," from
Twilight in Italy, and characteristically looking not for apparent meanings but for prophetic undercurrents, Lawrence finds that the play

> is the statement of the most significant philosophical position
> of the Renaissance. Hamlet is far more even than Orestes, his
> prototype, a mental creature, anti-physical, anti-sensual. The
> whole drama is the tragedy of the convulsed reaction of the
> mind from the flesh, of the spirit from the self, the reaction
> from the great aristocratic to the great democratic principle.
>   . . . At the bottom of his own soul Hamlet has decided that
> the Self in its supremacy, Father and King, must die. It is a
> suicidal decision for his involuntary soul to have arrived at. Yet
> it is inevitable. The great religious tide, which had been swell-
> ing all through the Middle Ages, had brought him there. . . .
>   . . . during the Middle Ages, struggling within this pagan,
> original transport . . . was a small dissatisfaction, a small con-
> trary desire. Amid the pomp of kings and popes was the child
> Jesus and the Madonna. . . . The monk rose up with his op-
> posite ecstasy, the Christian ecstasy. There was a death to die:
> the flesh, the self, must die, so that the spirit should rise again,
> immortal, eternal, infinite. . . .
>   At the Renaissance this great half-truth overcame the other
> great half-truth. The Christian Infinite . . . supplanted the old
> pagan Infinite. . . .
>   With Savonarola and Martin Luther the living Church ac-
> tually transformed itself, for the Roman church was still pagan
> . . . with Shakespeare the transformation reached the State
> also. The King, the Father . . . is rotten, corrupt. It must go.
> But Shakespeare was also the thing itself. Hence his horror,
> his frenzy, his self-loathing.
>   The King, the Emperor is killed in the soul of man, the old
> order of life is over, the old tree is dead at the root. So said
> Shakespeare. It was finally enacted in Cromwell. Charles I
> took up the old position of kingship by divine right.
>   Like Hamlet's father, he was blameless otherwise. But as

representative of the old form of life, which mankind now
hated with a frenzy, he must be cut down, removed. There
should be no king, no lords, no aristocrats. . . . And the *vital*
governing idea in the State has been this idea since Cromwell. . . .

Now this has failed. Now we say that the Christian Infinite
is not infinite. We are tempted, like Nietzsche, to return back
to the old pagan Infinite, to say that is supreme. . . .

What is really Absolute is the mystic Reason which con-
nects both natures of God. If we now wish to make a living
State, we must build it up to the idea of the Holy Spirit, the
supreme Relationship. . . .

The soliloquies of Hamlet are as deep as the soul can go in
one direction, and as sincere as the Holy Spirit itself in their
essence. But thank heaven, the bog into which Hamlet strug-
gled is almost surpassed.   [Pp. 93–102]

This seems to me a keen, even profound view of *Hamlet,* despite,
or because of, the enormous context into which the play is placed,
and I regret that my present concern, which is more the direction of
Lawrence's criticism than its content, does not permit me to dwell on
it. But something should be said at this point about the terminology,
which may be puzzling to someone not familiar with Lawrence.

It should be understood that categories such as Pagan Infinite and
Christian Infinite are antinomian tendencies in the collective psyche
and as such only roughly amenable to ordinary chronology. Thus
Lawrence, like Yeats, understands Christianity as a movement in the
psyche of mankind which originated before Christ but did not become
ascendant over its contrary until the Renaissance. The meaning of
such quasi-mystical terms becomes more concrete through the context:
Christian Infinite is aligned with mind, spirit, the democratic principle,
the Child Jesus and the Madonna, and is opposed to flesh, self, King,
Father, and the aristocratic principle. Understanding is complicated,
however, by Lawrence's tendency to shift his terms, as if, having
chosen them for their connotative richness, he is impatient with
their denotative inexactness.

The "Study of Thomas Hardy" introduces new terms for an extension of the argument, the most common of which are Law (for
Pagan Infinite) and Love (for Christian Infinite). The Renaissance is

still the pivotal moment, although Michelangelo is now the pivotal figure, probably because much of Lawrence's attention is centered on the visual arts. On one side stand Dürer and Botticelli, whose art is still rich in pagan ease; on the other, stand Correggio and Rembrandt, whose art has become increasingly tense and self-conscious. Around them on either side, in roughly chronological order, fall most of the leading artists of Western civilization, evincing in various proportions the complementary antinomies of Law and Love. But as he approaches the end of his long essay, Lawrence becomes less interested in contemplating some absolute structure than in revealing the prophetic implications of his argument:

> After Sue [Bridehead], after Dostoievsky's Idiot, after Turner's latest pictures, after the symbolist poetry of Mallarmé and the others, after the music of Debussy, there is no further possible utterance of the peace that passeth all understanding, the peace of God which is Perfect Knowledge. There is only silence beyond this.
>
> Just as after Plato, after Dante, after Raphael, there was no further utterance of the Absoluteness of the Law, of the Immutability of the Divine Conception.
>
> So that, as the great pause came over Greece, over Italy, after the Renaissance, when the Law had been uttered in its absoluteness, there comes over us now, now we have seen the purity of knowledge, the great, white, uninterrupted Light, infinite and eternal.
>
> But that is not the end. The two great conceptions, of Law and . . . Love, are not diverse and accidental but complementary. . . .
>
> . . . The greatest utterance of Love has given expression to Love as it is in relation to Law: so Rembrandt, Shakespeare, Shelley, Wordsworth, Goethe, Tolstoi. But beyond these there have been Turner, who suppressed the context of the Law; also there have been Dostoievsky, Hardy, Flaubert. These have shown Love in conflict with the Law, and only Death the resultant, no Reconciliation. . . .
>
> Now the aim of man remains to recognize and seek out the Holy Spirit, the Reconciler . . . [*P* 512–14]

Both essays envision a vast reconciliation, which Lawrence himself tried to embody in *The Rainbow,* on which he was working at this time. But after *The Rainbow*, or probably somewhat before it was completed—for the last half of that novel does not support dramat- ically the triumphant incantation in the very last paragraph—he abandoned the idea of imminent reconciliation and with it his faith in an eternal return. Having come to fear that civilization had passed a point of no return, he gave up his search for a supreme balance and, in the work of the next ten years, adopted a revolutionary strategy: the Christian-Democratic-Love mode must die so that a new life mode may emerge. He tried constantly to imagine the substance of that new mode, but his work of this period—for example, *Studies in Classic American Literature*—is less impressive for its revelation of the new than for its repudiation of the old. The essays of *Studies,* particularly the first two versions, read most persuasively as an anatomy of Fallen Man revealed by a Fallen Art. For art, in Lawrence's view, had degenerated from the original splendor of myth, as in the Old Testament, to legend, romance, and finally, "the personal plane . . . of art proper" (*SM* 124), just as the old vital sciences of alchemy, magic, and astrology had collapsed into fortune telling and a concern with personal fate. As for the major types of Fallen Man, *The Scarlet Letter,* as Lawrence read it, defined them: Hester is the pagan *magna mater* become destructive, because modern man worships instead of leading her; Chillingworth is her counterpart, the old male authority, but now "a shell, without passional belief"; Dimmesdale is modern man himself, cut off from a vital purpose and too weak to lead; and Pearl is, in embryo, the counterpart of Dimmesdale, the modern woman whose independent will has become hard and diabolical.

Having anatomized the modern condition as thoroughly as he could in *Studies* I and II (1917–20), "Education of the People" (1918), and *Fantasia* (1920), Lawrence devoted his prophetic energy between 1920 and 1925—i.e. between *Aaron's Rod* and *The Plumed Serpent*— to finding some way out, some viable new way of life. During this period he came as close as he ever did to superseding the idea of relationship itself. Maleness, which had begun to be violated by the Greeks in *Twilight in Italy,* and which was a name for the violator —now triumphant—in "Study of Thomas Hardy," is now restored to splendor. It becomes—especially in *The Plumed Serpent,* where it is called manhood—a name for the new whole, for the Holy Ghost of relationship itself. It is sometimes identified with the morning or the evening star, joining the opposites of night and day; sometimes it is the clue which joins the bird and the serpent, the spiritual and the sensual.[7]

After 1925 Lawrence's view of history tends to be less metaphysical and apocalyptic, more socio-psychological and nostalgic. Holy Spirit is converted into "vital sanity"; insanity, in fact, becomes the clear and present danger to civilization. In his characteristic literary criticism of this period Lawrence tries to distinguish wholesome from unwholesome art. His polemic is less often directed at the great in whom "error" is most vivid, more often at some broader based subversion of greatness, often called, in the jargon of the period, the "bourgeois" consciousness.

Lawrence's late reading of cultural history is summed up in the opening paragraphs of "Introduction to These Paintings":

> The reason the English produce so few paintings is not that they are, as a nation, devoid of a genuine feeling for visual art: though to look at their productions, and to look at the mess which has been made of actual English landscape, one might really conclude that they were, and leave it at that. But it is not the fault of the God that made them. They are made with aesthetic sensibilities the same as anybody else. The fault lies in the English attitude to life.
>
> The English, and the Americans following them, are paralyzed with fear. That is what thwarts and distorts the Anglo-Saxon existence, this paralysis of fear. It thwarts life, it distorts vision, and it strangles impulse: this overmastering fear. . . .
>
> It is an old fear, which seemed to dig in to the English soul at the time of the Renaissance. Nothing could be more lovely and fearless than Chaucer. But already Shakespeare is morbid with fear, fear of consequences. . . .
>
> What appeared to take full grip on the northern consciousness at the end of the sixteenth century was a terror, almost a horror of the sexual life. The Elizabethans, grand as we think them, started it. The real "mortal coil" in Hamlet is all sexual; the young man's horror of his mother's incest, sex carrying with it a wild and nameless terror which, it seems to me, it had never

7. Frederick Carter tells us that during this time Lawrence wanted to place the macrocosm in the microcosm, to make the individual as self-sufficient as possible (*Body Mystical*, p. 55).

carried before. Oedipus and Hamlet are very different in this respect. In Oedipus there is no recoil from sex itself: the Greek drama never shows that. The horror, when it is present in Greek tragedy, is against *destiny*, man caught in the toils of destiny. . . .

This, no doubt, is all in the course of the growth of the "spiritual-mental" consciousness, at the expense of the instinctive-intuitive consciousness. Man came to have his own body in horror, especially in its sexual implications: and so he began to suppress with all his might, his instinctive-intuitive consciousness, which is so radical, so physical, so sexual. Cavalier poetry, love poetry, is already devoid of body. Donne, after the exacerbated revulsion-attraction excitement of his earlier poetry, becomes a divine. "Drink to me only with thine eyes," sings the Cavalier: an expression incredible in Chaucer's poetry. "I could not love thee, dear, so much, loved I not honour more," sings the Cavalier lover. In Chaucer the "dear" and the "honour" would have been more or less identical.

. . . To the Restoration dramatist sex is, on the whole, a dirty business, but they more or less glory in the dirt. Fielding tries in vain to defend the Old Adam. Richardson with his calico purity and underclothing excitements sweeps all before him. Swift goes mad with sex and excrement revulsion. Sterne flings a bit of the same excrement humourously around. And physical consciousness gives a last song in Burns, and then is dead. Wordsworth, Keats, Shelley, the Brontës, are all postmortem poets.

. . . The essential instinctive-intuitive body is dead, and worshipped in death—all very unhealthy.   [*P* 551—52]

The argument of these pungent and perceptive paragraphs is similar to the one sixteen years earlier, but it is less symbolistic; it has more pretensions to historical exactness. Lawrence goes on to trace the cause of our fear of sex to the introduction of syphilis into Europe at the time of the Renaissance. And he intelligently confronts, if he does not quite nullify, likely objections: Why have the English produced a great modern literature but a less important body of painting, and why have the French, also exposed to syphilis, managed to produce important painting?

Lawrence observes that it is easier to escape the body in literature than in painting, for painting depends much more on the representation of substantial bodies and on the imaginative perception of their reality. English portraiture from the eighteenth century shows that the visual imagination has superseded the instinctive imagination: "The coat is really more important than the man. In Titian, in Velasquez, in Rembrandt, the people are there inside their clothes . . . and the clothes are imbued with the life of the individual, the gleam of the warm procreative body comes through all the time. . . . But modern people are nothing inside their garments." Blake is the exception. He "paints with real intuitional awareness and solid instinctive feeling . . . even if he sometimes makes [the body] a mere ideograph." When painting depends less on the representation of bodies, as in landscape, "the English exist and hold their own." But landscape "doesn't call up the more powerful responses of the human imagination. . . . There is no deep conflict . . . it is not confronted with any living, procreative body" (*P* 560–61).

Lawrence is almost as perceptive in explaining the greater success of French painting:

> In France it was more or less the same, but with a difference. The French, being more rational, decided that the body had its place, but that it should be rationalized. The Frenchman of today has the most reasonable and rationalized body possible. His conception of sex is basically hygienic. A certain amount of copulation is good for you. *Ça fait du bien au corps!* sums up the physical side of a Frenchman's idea of love, marriage, food, sport, and all the rest. Well, it's more sane, anyhow, than the Anglo-Saxon terrors. The Frenchman is afraid of syphilis and afraid of the procreative body, but not quite so deeply. He has known for a long time that you can take precautions. And he is not profoundly imaginative.   [*P* 562]

Impressionism and post-Impressionism are dead ends, extensions of what is unwholesome in the modern ideological climate—except, that is, for Cézanne, who becomes the "hero" of this essay. It was Cézanne who made the first effort, with very imperfect success—he painted mostly "his conflict and his failure, and the result is almost ridiculous"—to identify himself with his body and to rise in the flesh. "He rolled the stone from the mouth of the tomb" (*P* 563), precisely the phrase Lawrence had used in *Psychoanalysis and the Unconscious* to describe his own prophetic objective.

With his account of Cézanne, Lawrence carries his history of the

Fall as far back as history itself will permit—even farther, as we shall see in a moment. Beyond this the novelist or imaginative essayist can only give us images of unfallen or resurrected man, as in *Etruscan Places,* "The Man Who Died," and "A Propos of Lady Chatterley's Lover":

> The actual fact is that in Cézanne modern French art made its first tiny step back to real substance. . . . Cézanne's great effort was, as it were, to shove the apple away from him, and let it live of itself. It seems a small thing to do: yet it is the first real sign that man has made for several thousands of years that he is willing to admit that matter *actually exists.* Strange as it may seem, for thousands of years, in short, ever since the mythological "Fall," man has been preoccupied with . . . the denial of the existence of matter, and the proof that matter is only a form of spirit. . . .
>
> The history of our era is the nauseating and repulsive history of the crucifixion of the procreative body for the glorification of the spirit, the mental consciousness. Plato was an arch-priest of this crucifixion. Art, that handmaid, humbly and honestly served the vile deed, through three thousand years at least. The Renaissance put the spear through the side of the already crucified body, and syphilis put poison into the wound made by the imaginative spear. It took still three hundred years for the body to finish: but in the eighteenth century it became a corpse, with an abnormally active mind: and today it stinketh.
>
> We, dear readers, you and I, were born corpses. . . . All we know is shadows, even of apples. We are inside the tomb.
>
> [P 567–69]

·——————————·

Considering Lawrence's readings of history as a whole, we find a large measure of consistency in general purport and a large measure of inconsistency in detail. The nature of the Fall is fairly clear, but when exactly did it occur—at the time of Cromwell, Shakespeare, Michelangelo, Dante, Jesus, Plato, or still farther back? The Renaissance remains a crucial time, but in early Lawrence it is *the* turning point, whereas after 1925 it is more often a later phase of degeneration. In an essay and play of 1925 he went back to the biblical David, who had introduced a personal conception of God, to locate the origin of the Fall. In 1927 he opined that there had been a "great epoch" before 2000 B.C., "when man did not make war. . . . The self had not really become aware of itself, it had not yet separated itself off, the spirit was not yet born, so there was no internal conflict, and hence no permanent external conflict" (P 769). And finally, as we have seen in "Introduction to These Paintings" (1929), he drove himself out of history altogether, with the statement: "ever since the mythological 'Fall,' man has been preoccupied with . . . the denial of the existence of matter."

Foolish as some of this is, it testifies to the earnestness of Lawrence's commitment to a brave but virtually impossible task, which was to join his vision of a self-redeemed man and society to his awareness of psychological and social reality. But it is difficult to be satisfied with this kind of historiography. For one thing, actual figures cannot be fully enough separated from their historical contexts to become wholly functioning symbols in an individual design, however grand— a problem that is more acute when chronology is as freely handled as it is in Lawrence and Yeats. Then there is the curious notion of a gradual Fall. There is little difficulty in accepting the idea of overlapping or criss-crossing ideological currents. In fact, revolutions in thought and feeling *are* gradual and cumulative, however suddenly they seem to emerge. But the idea of a Fall in stages (Plato, Christ, Cromwell) is not very satisfying either as myth or history. Given the historical premises of the argument, Lawrence can never give it the autonomy of an artistic structure. It is astonishing how much useful insight it contains, how much light a powerful subjectivity can shed when it spreads itself over the panorama of fact, but the flux and diversity of actual history remains essentially intractable to the authority of myth. And finally, there is the amount of inconsistency, a problem peculiar to Lawrence.

Lawrence tends to exceed his contemporaries both in earnestness of belief and in skeptical resistance to belief, which makes his myth of the Fall both more stark and more inconsistent. His skepticism, at bottom a kind of uncompromising empiricism, makes him unwilling to imagine an ideality beyond what he felt at any time to be possible, causing him to push farther and farther away his dream of a perfect art and a perfect society as his personal hope for wholeness and perfection of being came to seem more frail. His earnestness comes

from his intense desire for change, a desire that suppressed any temptation to share T. E. Hulme's belief that "orientation to action debars
entry into the pure flux of imagination."[8]

We will be in a better position to evaluate Lawrence's particular
historical myth if we take a moment to clarify it further through
direct contrast to Hulme's, a contrast that interestingly points up what
radically different ideologies could be fitted to the same intellectual
framework and derived from the same intellectual dilemma.

Hulme traced a shift at the time of the Renaissance from a
"life-denying" mode of consciousness, which he admired, to a "life-
worshipping" one, which he deplored. Lawrence would make the
very same statement with exactly reversed terms! Both were attracted
to the religious and impersonal qualities of medieval art and life, and
both deplored the secularism, the democracy, the self-sufficient in-
dividualism of the modern era. But Hulme criticized the art produced
since the Renaissance as vitalistic and life-affirming, while Lawrence
criticized it as personal and life-denying. Hulme believed art should
aspire to the condition of geometry and thought he saw in Cézanne
an art that approached such an ideal. Lawrence execrated this ideal,
but also thought he saw in Cézanne the promise of a more desirable
art: in his view Cézanne's geometrism signified an effort to escape
the clichés of representational art and to restore the lost life of the
body.

Hulme and Lawrence were both prompted by a religious impulse
in their efforts to resolve their dilemma, but the impulse of the one
was neo-orthodox, that of the other, Romantic. The real difference,
I think, is that the heightened naturalism of Romantic faith enabled
Lawrence to emphasize human powers and to reconcile a religious
with an heroic conception of man, whereas Hulme's belief in a realm
of absolute value absolutely beyond man inevitably led him to regard
religious and heroic conceptions of man as incompatible. Hulme was
antihumanistic, Lawrence was "metahumanistic."

Returning, then, to the problem of Lawrence's excesses and in-
consistencies, we must admit that in some sense they make his
historical myth less satisfactory than, say, Eliot's or Yeats'. Yet Eliot's

8. T. E. Hulme, *Speculations* (New York, 1962), p. 154. I draw on these
essays passim in the following paragraphs.

famous "dissociation of sensibility" theory, though ingenious and interesting, and though still widely regarded as "proved," is inherently neither more nor less true than Lawrence's theory, only more likely to mislead. Is it really anything more than an anti-Protestant or anti-modern polemic, expressing nostalgia for an age of traditional faith, public myth, and aristocratic social values? Are not feeling and thought combined in the Romantic poets as much as in Donne? It is ironical, by the way, that the more candid polemic against Protestantism should come from Lawrence, whose Protestantism was so radical that it was turned even against itself, very much as Shaw's radical Protestant vision in *Saint Joan* seeks for itself a Catholic base. As for Yeats, he proposes a frankly mythical view of history. His scheme is certainly more systematic and aesthetically satisfying than Lawrence's, but is relatively untroubled by a sense of historical reality. A cyclical view of history, such as Yeats held, was congenial to an intellectual temper like Lawrence's and is articulate in his work, but insofar as it released man from the burden of history and from the responsibility of changing it, it would have to be rejected.

Mircea Eliade, arguing for a Christian view of history, believes that Romantic self-transcendence is impossible and that we need myth because it is "our only resistance to the terror of events."[9] Philip Rahv, taking a more or less Freudian view, scorns the "mythomania" of modern criticism as "an escape from history."[1] Lawrence seemed to lean now one way, now the other, and sometimes both ways at the same time. What this abrasive combination came down to in practice was that, while Lawrence consistently maintained a belief in a potential perfection within history, he was compelled again and again to return to the bare idea of potentiality.

9. Mircea Eliade, *The Myth of the Eternal Return*, trans. Willard Trask (New York, 1954), p. 152.
1. Philip Rahv, "Criticism and Boredom," *New Statesman*, 56, No. 1434 (1958), 311.

6

Heroes of Death and Heroes of Rebirth

Lawrence's argument of an historical Fall should not blind us to the fact that all of his villains—even Plato and Jesus—are also heroes. Indeed, they could not otherwise have become villains. They are the points in history at which "error" has been most vividly expressed. Moreover, their error is relative to the one thing needful for our day. Relative to their own day, they were simply heroes. They released spiritual power into the world; they extended human consciousness, even if their present influence is to be deplored. This was particularly true of Jesus and Paul, who gave humanity a psychic capital it has taken almost two thousand years to spend. Lawrence was fascinated by the conversion of Paul and confessed that he himself would have been a Christian had he lived at the beginning of the Christian era (*P* 734). He was also fascinated by the symbol of Jesus as fish or whale, taking it to represent the plunge into the sea of the unknown toward a creative rebirth (*S* 174).

Lawrence recognized as vital both spiritual and practical power; he recognized as heroes both men of thought and men of action. But the "thought-adventurers" were far more important to him, for he wanted a revolution of consciousness more than one of social forms, and he found men of action insensitive (*P* 358). He liked to compare the thought-adventurer, particularly the artist, to the growing tip of a tree, his society to the flowing sap in the trunk. The image works two ways: to suggest his distance from his society and to suggest his prophetic function. It is his challenge as well as his doom to live at the limits of consciousness and to extend those limits as far as he is able.

Dark gods and a religion of the blood notwithstanding, extensive consciousness is a central emphasis in Lawrence's work. He saw no way of getting back to full being except by going forward through knowing and self-realization. Complete self-realization was virtually unattainable: "A human being who was completely himself has never even been conceived. The great Goethe was half-born, Shakespeare the same, Napoleon only a third-born. And most people are hardly born at all, into individual consciousness" (*P* 131).[1] But it was the ideal. An interesting consequence of this emphasis is that Lawrence, unlike some earlier Romantics, deglamourized the child. The less-conscious child was even more liable to automatism than the adult. It was on the larger consciousness of the advanced mind and the advanced civilization that Lawrence pinned his prophetic hopes.

His view of the present vis-à-vis the past is, then, both pessimistic and optimistic. "Man always deteriorates" (*P* 299), but "brave men are forever born" (*P* 121). "Everything human degenerates, from religion downwards, and must be renewed and revived" (*Apoc.* 172). It is rather like Yeats' "All things fall and are built again / And those that build them again are gay." The words "dawn" and "morning" were charged for him, as they were for Thoreau, with the deepest glamour, representing both the heroic ages of earlier times and the human potentiality in the present, "the infinite expectation of the dawn."[2]

Perhaps just because the past was so seductive to him, he warns us frequently that we can't go back. Visionary optimism constantly checks in Lawrence the attitude of Romantic nostalgia. One of his most poignant evocations of vanished glamour is to be found in his preface to Maurice Magnus' *Memoirs of the Foreign Legion*. Recreating his visit to an Italian monastery rooted in the atmosphere of the Middle

---

1. Cf. Thoreau: "I have never met a man who was quite awake. How could I have looked him in the face?" *Walden* (New York, 1958), p. 73. Jessie Chambers tells us that Lawrence as a youth read *Walden* and was "wildly enthusiastic" (*A Personal Record*, p. 101).

2. Ibid., p. 126.

Ages, his first love among past periods and a lasting one, Lawrence is suddenly and rather inexplicably beset by claustrophobia:

> "The past, the past. The beautiful, the wonderful past, it seems to prey on my heart, I can't bear it". . . . Both worlds were agony to me. But here, on the mountain top, was the worst: the past, the poignancy of the not-quite-dead past. "I think one's got to go through with life down there—get somewhere beyond it. One can't go back," I said to him.[3]

It is, I think, the past cut off from the present, rather than related to it in a living tradition, that oppresses him in the monastery.

In an essay on Galsworthy, Lawrence makes a distinction between tradition and convention:

> There is a tremendous difference between the two things. To carry on a tradition you must add something to the tradition. But to keep up a convention needs only the monotonous persistency of a parasite, the endless endurance of the craven, those who fear life because they are not alive, and who cannot die because they cannot live—the social beings.   [*P* 543]

The distinction itself is conventional enough, but it indicates something of which the reader of Lawrence needs to be reminded. For by and large it was not tradition that was objectionable to him: he scolded the futurists for wanting "to deny every scrap of tradition and experience" (*L* 196); and he ridiculed Shaw, "who rose up in a day," for dismissing the slowly accumulated wisdom of the Catholic Church ("A Propos" 102 ff.). Rather, he objected to a habit of mind that reverence for tradition tended to inculcate, a habit of "persisting in an old attitude toward some important relationship which, in the course of time, has changed its nature" (*R* 161). At times he welcomed cataclysm, but never as a final goal. "Catastrophe alone never helped man. The only thing that ever avails is the living adventurous spark in the souls of men" (*P* 733). Destruction went hand in hand with continuity. "A deluge presupposes a Noah and an Ark" (*P* 734). One of his heroes was Attila, "a creator in wrath" (*P* 89). But he was equally fascinated by Noah and the medieval monks: they carried on

3. Reprinted in *The Noble Savage* (New York, Meridian periodical, No. 2, 1960), p. 207.

the light of consciousness during a time when it was almost extinguished. "Man is a thought-adventurer" (*AA* 190); we "are transmitters" (*CP* 449). These characteristic formulations indicate an important emphasis. Lawrence's enormous faith in the new (and the word has incantatory power for him)[4] is a measure of his passionate engagement with the present and of his sense of responsibility for the future.

In "The Reality of Peace" (1917), one of his better speculative essays, Lawrence distinguishes three classes of men: heroes of death, heroes of rebirth, and sheep. "Peace," the essay begins, "is the state of fulfilling the deepest desire of the soul." Our fulfillment may at one time require those who understand "according to death" and at another time those who understand "according to life"—the heroes of death and the heroes of rebirth, the Destroyers and Preservers, the Creators in Wrath and the Creators in Love. The burden of the essay is that we must banish fear by accepting all our vital desires, destructive as well as constructive, for both are necessary to creation and are part of the continuous cycle of death and rebirth. What Lawrence's heroes had in common was the courage to undergo vital death. In this they were to be distinguished on the one hand from sentimentalizers, who preserved and even made alluring the dead forms of consciousness, and on the other hand, from those stoics, such as the Red Indian or the Jew, who held themselves "aloof from change"; both merged with the "sheep," "the social beings," those "who cannot die because they cannot live" (*P* 669–94 passim).

I find the classifications "heroes of death" and "heroes of rebirth" useful for structuring a synoptic view of Lawrence's ideological criticism of nineteenth- and twentieth-century literature, although we should remember that all artists are to some extent both kinds of heroes, since death implies rebirth, and rebirth is impossible without death.

4. He uses the word "new" with remarkable frequency and intensity. Taking the 115 pieces in *Phoenix* as a fair sampling of his critical prose, we discover that 41 of them contain the word in an emphatic sense in the last paragraph, usually in the last sentence, and that 68 of them end with at least the idea of the new.

Heroes of Death and Heroes of Rebirth

Lawrence's heroes of death may be divided into two groups: first, those artists, usually of the nineteenth century, who more or less unconsciously burn down the dead forms by what might be called essential tragedy; and second, those artists, usually of the twentieth century, who more or less consciously burn out the dead forms by means of essential satire.

Chief among the first group are Hardy, Tolstoi, Dostoevsky, Poe, Hawthorne, Melville, and Whitman. Hardy and Tolstoi, as we have seen, revealed the tragic imbalance of physical and spiritual in the collective psyche. Hawthorne, Melville, and Whitman had the most vivid sense of the doom of the "white consciousness." The critic's prophetic reading of Dostoevsky and Poe is more ambiguous. *The Idiot* and "Ligeia" are profound exposures of the bankruptcy of the egoistic love-ideal. But Lawrence wavers as to whether the artistic impulse that informs them is truly physical and sensual or merely nervous and intellectual, as to whether it is the needed reduction *of* the ego or merely reduction *within* the ego. He called them sensationalists, an equivocal term in Lawrence, as we can see from the following passage:

> Poe shows us the first vivid, seething reduction of the psyche, the first convulsive spasm that sets in the human soul, when the last impulse of creative love, creative conjunction, is finished. . . .
> For men who are born at the end of a great era or epoch nothing remains but the seething reduction back to the elements; just as for a tree in autumn nothing remains but the strangling-off of the leaves and the strange decomposition and arrest of the sap. . . . The process is slow and bitter and beautiful, too. But the beauty has its spark in anguish; it is the strange, expiring cry, the phosphorescence of decay. . . .
> Yet Poe is hardly an artist. He is rather a supreme scientist. Art displays the movements of the pristine self, the living conjunction or communion between the self and its context. Even in tragedy self meets self in supreme conjunction, a communion of passionate or creative death. But in Poe the self is finished, already stark. It would be true to say that Poe had no soul. He lives in the post-mortem reality, a living dead. He reveals the after-effects of life, the processes of organic disintegration. Arrested in himself, he cannot realize self or soul in any other

115

human being. For him the vital world is the sensational world.
He is not sensual, he is sensational. The difference between
these two is the difference between growth and decay. [*S* I, 106–08]

Sensationalism is the reduction of consciousness which could prove
valuable "if it break the egoistic will and release the other flow"
(*R* 68), but which might prove only a cul-de-sac if the artist is
trapped by his fascination with the very process of reduction.

Lawrence seemed less able to discover essential tragedy in his
contemporaries, perhaps because he thought the time was too late.
As early as 1912 he had found Thomas Mann, in *Death in Venice,*
"so late" in teaching us "to be . . . aware of the fulsomeness of life"
(*P* 312–13). Contemporary tragedy should be "a great kick at misery"
(*L* 64). It must become overtly critical, for "the world needs criticizing
to death today" (*Lady Chatterley's Lover,* chap. 4).

Contemporary writers in whom he found this kind of essential
satire were: Maurice Magnus (*Memoirs of the Foreign Legion*);
Frederick Rolfe, alias Baron Corvo (*Hadrian the Seventh*); John Dos
Passos (*Manhattan Transfer* and *Three Soldiers*); Ernest Hemingway
(*In Our Time*); Edward Dahlberg (*Bottom Dogs*); and Aldous Huxley
(*Point Counter Point*). Lawrence did not exactly *like* this work, but
he valued it for its repudiative force. He observes in almost every
case that he is glad to have read the book in question and hopes it
is the last book of its kind that will have to be written. This becomes
a little tedious, but Lawrence was neither going to surrender his hope
nor claim a victory that had not actually been won.

These writers, he felt, succeeded in going "beyond tragedy to
howl and protest" (*P* 270). They were not ushering in the hoped-for
posttragic age, but because repulsiveness and disintegration were
real elements in modern life, howl and protest were genuine attitudes.
The seal of genuineness in the literature of repudiation is its lack
of sentimentality. The sentimentalist tries to tell us that terrible experiences are really not so terrible. He thus "glorifies corrupt feelings"
(*P* 550). Galsworthy, for instance, almost writes essential satire in
The Forsyte Saga, but he turns it off into sentimentalism: "This is
the final philosophy of it all. 'Things happen, but we bob up.' Very
well, then, write the book in that key, the keynote of a frank old
cynic. There's no point in sentimentalizing it and being a sneaking old

cynic. Why pour out masses of feeling that pretend to be genuine and then turn it off with: 'Things happen, but we bob up'?" (*P* 550) But Magnus, Dos Passos, Hemingway, Dahlberg, and Huxley expose the sordidness of modern experience without either sentimentalizing it or trying to ennoble it into tragedy.

Genuinely felt repudiation requires courage, because the writer must carry his consciousness through the painful or ugly experience that is being repudiated. This Lawrence finely explains in his introduction to Magnus' *Memoirs:*

> Let him have his place, let his word be heard. He went through vile experiences: he looked them in the face, braved them through, and kept his manhood in spite of them. For manhood is a strange quality, to be found in human rats as well as in hot-blooded men. M[agnus] carried the human consciousness through circumstances which would have been too much for me. I would rather have died than be so humiliated, I could never have borne it. Other men, I know, went through worse things in the war. But then, horrors, like pain, are their own anaesthetic. Men lose normal consciousness, and go through in a sort of delirium. . . . There are certain things which are so bitter, so horrible, that the contemporaries just cannot know them, cannot contemplate them. So it is with a great deal of the last war. It was so foul, and humanity in Europe fell suddenly into such ignominy and inhuman ghastliness, that we shall *never fully* realize what it was. We just cannot bear it. We haven't the soul-strength to contemplate it.
>
> And yet, humanity can only finally conquer by realizing. It is human destiny, since Man fell into consciousness and self-consciousness, that we can only go forward step by step through realization, full, bitter, conscious realization. This is true of all the great terrors and agonies and anguishes of life: sex, and war, and even crime. When Flaubert in his story . . . makes his saint kiss the leper, and naked clasp the leprous awful body against his own, that is what we must do. It is the great command, *Know Thyself.* . . . We have to take the disease into our consciousness and let it go through our soul, like some virus. We have got to realize. And then we can surpass.[5]

5. *The Noble Savage*, No. 2, pp. 248–49. The courageous "human rat" ("an extreme of impurity that is pure") is a persistent figure in the Lawrencean mythology: other examples are Loerke in *Women in Love* and Michaelis in

Chapter Six

Satire, then, though more self-conscious than tragedy, can be passionate or essential enough to have therapeutic value. "Even satire," Lawrence noted in *Lady Chatterley's Lover*, "is a form of sympathy. It is the way our sympathy flows and recoils that really determines our lives. And here lies the vast importance of the novel, properly handled. It can inform and lead into new places the flow of our sympathetic consciousness, and it can lead our sympathy away in recoil from things gone dead" (chap. 9).[6]

In contrast to this twentieth-century literature of repudiation stood the twentieth-century literature of negation, which was represented chiefly by Proust and Joyce. It signified a surrender of the artist's prophetic function and a retreat into what the critic called "aestheticism," a rubric that covers such Lawrencean phrases as the "would-be," the "warmed over," "conceit," "stunts," "self-importance," "self-consciousness picked into such fine bits that the bits are most of them invisible." Joyce and Proust, along with avant-garde art in general—e.g. cubist art, which "murdered the bowels of compassion in a man"

Lady Chatterley's Lover. Their strength is their private repudiation of conventional illusions; their weakness is their tendency to take satisfaction in a degrading separate peace, to become cynics, as little able as sentimentalists to lead us ahead. Here the strength is emphasized.

Lawrence, we remember, takes a different attitude toward Flaubert's St. Julien in his essay on Whitman (*Studies* III). There, the embrace of the leper was instanced as false sympathy, a failure of discrimination. Both points of view are characteristic, and it would be a labor of little purpose to try to reconcile them.

6. At times Lawrence seems to have in mind a distinction between a true kind of satire arising from genuine compassion and wrath and another kind which is mere nervous and intellectual reaction. Thus Huxley, Dahlberg, and Hemingway seem to have truly exposed the spiritual emptiness of their age, while Wells in *The World of William Clissold* is criticized for lacking "one gleam of sympathy with anything, one breath of passionate rebellion" (P 349) and socialist art is condemned as "a misdemeanor to anyone with a spark of natural balance" (*The Plumed Serpent*, chap. 3). But the distinction becomes rather elusive at times, as when Lawrence condemns criticizing as a barren mental activity which "severs the organic connection" and in the next breath asserts that "the world needs criticizing to death today" (*Lady Chatterley's Lover*, chap. 4). The truth is that in his later years, particularly the period of the verses called *Nettles*, Lawrence's own satire tended to be mere nervous and intellectual reaction, in spite of his continued allegiance to genuine compassion and wrath.

(*Lady Chatterley's Lover,* chap. 18)—committed a kind of double sin: they surrendered to the Zeitgeist instead of trying to transcend it, and they prided themselves on those very qualities, extreme self-consciousness and complexity of artifice, which destroyed natural touch and natural balance.

With a kind of Tolstoian or Ruskinian aesthetic puritanism, Lawrence became during the twenties increasingly intolerant of the artificial and monumental. The Elizabethans with their poetic conceits seemed "upholstered" (*Lady Chatterley's Lover,* chap. 8). Greek art contained an element of abstraction, of inhumanity, in contrast to the exemplary Etruscan art, the beauty of which was "not so pure as the Greek, but more ample," reflecting a people who knew how to preserve "the natural humour" of life and "the sense of touch," a people who could make the phallus a part of daily living without taking self-conscious attitudes; their art knew how to be "ordinary" without being "commonplace" (*Etruscan Places,* passim).[7]

To make a category of Lawrence's modern heroes of rebirth is to call attention to his difficulty in concretizing the new era, for we can only number among them: Cooper, in whom, the critic admits, the yearning myth is somewhat superficially felt; Whitman, whose prophetic meaning, as we shall see, is largely superimposed by the critic; and among contemporaries—apart from Cézanne—Leo Shestov and V. V. Rozanov. His most strenuous efforts of this kind are the essays on Cooper and Whitman.

Lawrence found in the progression of Cooper's Leatherstocking novels a myth-meaning that epitomized his thesis in *Studies:* Natty Bumppo goes from age, in *Pioneers,* to youth, in *Deerslayer,* as America itself seeks to slough off its old psyche and develop a new one. The more Cooper departs from historical actuality and moves toward myth, the more "he expands into significance." So it is in *Deerslayer* that Lawrence finds the deepest meaning.

In *Studies* I and to some extent in *Studies* III, Lawrence emphasizes "the immortal friendship of Chingachgook and Natty Bumppo," through which Cooper "dreamed the nucleus of a new society . . . a new relationship, a stark, stripped human relationship of two men,

---

7. Ordinary, as opposed to commonplace, was almost always a good word for Lawrence. Throughout *Sons and Lovers* Miriam is criticized for not being ordinary enough, for working up her feelings through her will.

deeper than the deeps of sex." In most of the latter essay, however, he subordinates the friendship idea and emphasizes the stark, enduring figure of Deerslayer preserving his integrity. But even this is presented with a good deal of skeptical undercutting, and we find at the end of the essay that Natty has not exactly made a new move but has become ready to make one:

> [Natty] is not going to be mastered. A philosophic old soul, he does not give much for the temptation of sex. Probably he dies virgin.
> And he is right of it. Rather than be dragged into a false heat of deliberate sensuality, he will remain alone. . . . So he will preserve his integrity, and remain alone in the flesh. . . .
> He lets his consciousness penetrate in loneliness into the new continent. His contacts are not human. . . . His one meeting is with Chingachgook, and this meeting is silent, reserved, across an unpassable distance. . . .
> He says "hurt nothing unless you're forced to." And yet he lives by death, by killing the wild things of the air and earth.
> It's not good enough.
> But you have there the myth of the essential America. All the other stuff, the love, the democracy, the floundering into lust, is a sort of by-play. . . .
> This is the very intrinsic-most American. . . . And when *this* man breaks from his static isolation, and makes a new move, then look out, something will be happening.   [*S* 71–73]

But the full weight of Lawrence's visionary yearning in *Studies* is applied to Whitman. The effort was not quite successful, as we shall see in the next chapter, but it is not difficult to see why he wanted to cast Whitman as the hero of the book. Whitman must have seemed to Lawrence, like the about-to-be-created Don Ramon, a Lord of the Two Ways, combining an understanding according to death with an understanding according to rebirth: the phoenix incarnate.

The Russians Shestov and Rozanov are less conspicuous figures in the Lawrencean pantheon. In the thematic title of Shestov's *All Things Are Possible* (for a translation of which he wrote a brief preface in 1920), Lawrence found an echo of one of his own abiding convictions, and he called it, "when dressed up in a little comely language, a real ideal, that will last us for a new, long epoch" (*P* 216). But the book seems to have made no lasting impression on him. He has forgotten it seven years later when, in reviewing Rozanov's *Solitaria* and *The Apocalypse of Our Times,* he praises the author as "the first Russian . . . who has ever said anything to me." Rozanov "is the first to see that immortality is in the vividness of life, not in the loss of life. . . . he has more or less recovered the genuine pagan vision, the phallic vision, and with those eyes he looks, in amazement and consternation, on the mess of Christianity. . . . Rozanov matters, for the future" (*P* 369–71).

One striking thing about Lawrence's contemporary answerers is that they are diarists or essayists; the new word is presented more as statement than as imaginative experience, which, by the critic's own standards, would rob it of much of its therapeutic potential. Lawrence, I think, knew this, for he did not mention these writers outside of the essays devoted to them. Another striking thing—and it is probably not accidental—is that his modern heroes of rebirth are Americans and Russians. "Two bodies of modern literature," he wrote in the foreword to *Studies,* "have come to a real verge: the Russian and the American" (*S* 8). They were nearer psychic revolution and thus made the deepest appeal to his prophetic imagination.

There is a complementary side to the critic's strong orientation to the future: his deep attraction to pre-fallen imaginative worlds, represented chiefly by Homer's *Odyssey* and by the tales of Giovanni Verga. We can gain a clearer understanding of the importance Lawrence attached to the Northern consciousness, and to the Russians and Americans in particular, if we sketch in his view of Verga, its true opposite.

The error of Verga's art—"the emotional-democratic vision," expressed through the theme of "the tragic fate of the poor"—was borrowed from the North and can be put aside. That done, we are left with a rich sense of physical life and a vision of the old world before the fall into self-consciousness:

> The Sicilian, in our sense of the word, doesn't have any soul. He just hasn't got our sort of subjective consciousness. . . .
> The self-tortured Jesus, the self-tortured Hamlet, simply doesn't exist. Why should a man torture himself? Gesualdo would ask in amazement. Aren't there scoundrels enough in the world to torture him? . . .

Chapter Six

So that in *Mastro-don Gesualdo* you have the very antithesis of what you get in *The Brothers Karamazov*. Anything more un-Russian than Verga it would be hard to imagine: save Homer. Yet Verga has the same sort of pity as the Russians. And with the Russians, he is a realist. He won't have heroes, nor appeals to gods above nor below.

. . . if you come to think of it, Gesualdo Motta might really be a Greek in modern setting, except that he is not intellectual. But this many Greeks were not. And he has the energy, the quickness, the vividness of the Greek, the same vivid passion for wealth, the same ambition, the same lack of scruples, the same queer openness, without ever really committing himself. . . .

He is Greek above all in not having any soul or lofty ideals. The Greeks were far more bent on making an audacious, splendid impression than on fulfilling some noble purpose. They loved the splendid look of a thing, the splendid ring of words. Even tragedy was to them a grand gesture, rather than something to mope over. Peak and pine they would not, and unless some Fury pursued them to punish them for their sins, they cared not a straw for sins: their own or anyone else's. . . .

Gesualdo . . . was remorselessly and relentlessly objective, like all people that belong to the sun. In the sun men are objective, in the mist and snow, subjective. . . .

How utterly different it is from Russia, where the people are always—in the books—expanding to one another, and pouring out tea and their souls to one another all night long. . . .

[Sicily] seems to some people dark and squalid and brutal and boring. . . . But if you have any physical feeling for life, apart from nervous feelings such as the Russians have, nerves, nerves—if you have any appreciation for the southern way of life, then what a strange, deep fascination there is in *Mastro-don Gesualdo!* . . .

It is only when they bunch together as citizens that they are squalid. In the countryside, they are portentous and subtle, like the wanderers in the Odyssey. And their relations are all curious and immediate, objective. They are so little aware of themselves, and so much aware of their own effects.

It all depends on what you are looking for. Gesualdo's lifelong love-affair with Diodata is, according to our ideas, quite impossible. He puts no value on sentiment at all: or almost none: again a real Greek. Yet there is a strange forlorn beauty in it, impersonal, a bit like Rachel or Rebecca. It is of the old, old world, when man is aware of his own belongings, acutely, but only dimly aware of his own feelings. And feelings you are not aware of, you don't have.

Gesualdo seems so potent, so full of potency. Yet nothing emerges, and he never says anything. It is the very reverse of the Russians, who talk and talk, out of impotence.

And you have a wretched, realistic kind of tragedy for the end. And you feel, perhaps the book was all about nothing, and Gesualdo wasn't worth the labour of Verga.

But that is because we are spiritual snobs, and think, because a man can fume with 'To be or not to be,' therefore he is a person to be taken account of. Poor Gesualdo had never heard of: To be or not to be, and he wouldn't have taken any notice if he had. He lived blindly, with the impetuosity of blood and muscles, sagacity and will, and he never woke up to himself. Whether he would have been any better for waking up to himself, who knows! [*P* 228–31]

In this rather plausible mixture of sociology, anthropology, and literary criticism Lawrence gives us a fair idea of the kind of thing he was after. Yet the whole passage is a little curious: it is characteristic, but there is so much weaving and self-questioning that we feel he is half trying to convince himself. The reason for this, I think, is that, while Lawrence was deeply attracted to the southern way of life and the old world, he did not believe that Verga's vision constituted an immediate, realizable alternative for modern man. It might be an ultimate goal, but it could not help us to take the next step. The question with which the passage ends is not as rhetorical as it may seem; Lawrence himself is recoiling a little from the limitations of Gesualdo's consciousness. It is worth noting that he elaborates this life-ideal more often out of fiction than in it, notably in *Etruscan Places* and "A Propos of Lady Chatterley's Lover." We get some of it in the first part of *The Rainbow,* though in reference to a past generation; in some tales, though often ironically; in parts of *Lady Chatterley's Lover,* though more conceptually than dramatically. In short, Lawrence tended to regard Verga's view of life nostalgically, as idyll.

He felt kindlier toward Verga and toward the "natural ease" of

Mediterranean culture generally, but he felt more closely identified with the ultraconscious Russians and Americans: with Dostoevsky ("I even feel a sort of subterranean love" for him), who "never wanted anybody to love him" (*SL* 108); and with Melville, who was "too keen and abstract," "over the border," "beyond humanity."

Of the Americans, Melville seems to have made the profoundest impression upon him. Melville's vision and Verga's were at opposite extremes, yet touched in being so. Verga's "brown-eyed" Old World before the Fall was impersonal in one way, Melville's ultramodern world was impersonal in another.

> Brown eyed people are, as it were, like the earth, which is tissue of bygone life, organic, compound. In blue eyes there is sun and rain and abstract uncreate element, water, ice, air, space, but not humanity. . . . Melville is like a Viking going home to the sea, encumbered with age and memories, and a sort of accomplished despair, almost madness. For he cannot accept humanity. . . . The great Northern cycle of which he is the returning unit has almost completed its round, accomplished itself. . . . Human life won't do. He turns back to the elements. [*S* 142–43]

This view of life is apocalyptic rather than idyllic. And Lawrence's resistance to *it* is dramatic rather than skeptical: Melville, like all demonic things, is "strange," "uncanny," "repulsive."

We are touching on what Lawrence called "the spirit of place," the idea that "Some peculiar potentiality attaches to every distinct region of the earth's surface" (*SM* 20) and that art inevitably expresses this spirit. To complete our study of Lawrence's view of cultural history, we need to give this important idea some independent consideration.

⊹————————————⊹

Like many northern European writers, Lawrence was fascinated by the South and the Latin temperament, and he soon worked up this traditional contrast into a complex psycho-geography. The South he associated with sensual consciousness, the North with spiritual consciousness. As we have seen, either side may be criticized insofar as it seeks to be exclusive, although Lawrence's tendency is to think of the former as nearer to the truth than the latter. But in the early *Twilight in Italy* they are the two poles. The South tends to believe only in Flesh, the North only in Spirit. The South worships the body as the whole of the creative divinity; the North suppresses the body or, like Strindberg and Ibsen, exalts it "obscenely" in the mind. The more revolutionary perspective he came to adopt opened up new alternatives. On the one hand, the South represents the nontragic pre-Renaissance sense of life and the objective, nonintellectual consciousness belonging to people whose divinity is the sun; and the North represents the tragic post-Renaissance sense of life and the subjective, intellectual consciousness belonging to people whose divinity is the moon. But, on the other hand, the South, insofar as it adheres to an older consciousness, is resistant to the progress of man's necessary thought-adventure: "A long-clinched timeless embrace has been the history of Italian art since Raphael" (*P* 464). The spirit of the South is abnegation, of the North aspiration (*P* 33). So, in the modern era, the North has been more instrumental in carrying the consciousness forward.[8]

Italy was always dear to Lawrence, but for the reasons indicated, he did not pursue his thought-adventure very ardently through Italian culture. Nor, for different reasons, did he particularly interest himself in either French or German culture. He was always more or less hostile to the French spirit; it seemed too rationalized and sophisticated to be either lovely in itself, like the Italian, or promising for the future, like the Russian and American. About the German spirit he was— perhaps like all of us—ambivalent. He disliked its militarism, but in the curious abstractness of its people he sometimes found glimpses of the old barbarian and of "another world of men." The Teutonic spirit, unlike the Latin, was more deeply individual than social, and thus had more revolutionary potential (*P* 128–32).

8. When he comments on individual artists, Lawrence will usually discover some degree of dynamic tension between the opposing forces. In Dante and Michelangelo there was flesh-rootedness and the idealist's revolt from this, an incipient tragic dilemma (*P* 403). In Whitman, Cézanne, and other artists of the modern and Northern sensibility, there was the predominant spirit-consciousness and the desperate effort to recover the flesh. When he takes the grand view, the tension of forces is often displaced to the regions themselves, most apparent in his discussion of America's spirit of place.

Lawrence is more antagonistic toward Russian culture than toward any other in Europe, but at the same time more interested in its future. Some uncertainty of feeling is apparent, I think, in the foreword to *Studies:* "Two bodies of modern literature seem to me to have come to a real verge: the Russian and the American. . . . The European moderns are all *trying* to be extreme. The great Americans . . . just were it" (*S* 8). Are the Russians trying to be extreme and failing, or trying and succeeding? Failing seems to be the usual verdict, as in this letter of 1916:

> I got Sportsman's Sketches and have read them. No, I don't like Turgenev very much; he seems so very critical, like Katherine Mansfield, and also a sort of male old maid. It amazes me that we have bowed down and worshipped these foreigners as we have. Their art is so clumsy, really, and clayey, compared with our own. I read "Deerslayer" just before the Turgenev. And I can tell you what a comedown it was, from the pure and exquisite art of . . . Cooper—whom we count nobody—to the journalistic bludgeonings of Turgenev. They are all—Turgenev, Tolstoi, Dostoevsky, Maupassant, Flaubert —so very *obvious* and coarse, beside the lovely, mature and sensitive art of . . . Cooper or Hardy. It seems to me that our English art, at its best, is by far the subtlest and loveliest and most perfect in the world. But it is characteristic of a highly de-veloped nation to bow down to that which is more gross and raw and affected. [*SL* 145]

Both Russian and American art revealed the effects of too sudden cultural development (*P* 390), but Lawrence often implies that Russian art was not in the true line of development. It was "a surgical outcry" against the imposition of Western ideas, not "the flowering of a race." It was not genuine or spontaneous, only "horrifying or marvellous, lacerating at first; but when we get used to it, not really so profound, not really ultimate, a little extraneous" (*P* 215). Classic American literature, however, was really ultimate. It "is *older* than our English. The tree did not become new, which was transplanted. It only ran more swiftly into age, impersonal, nonhuman almost. But how good these books are!" (*SL* 141)

The Russian Revolution Lawrence usually viewed as a collapse into materialism and antilife, but it interested him too as a current and not entirely determinable experiment. Socialism in general and Bolshevism in particular are subjects in every novel from *Aaron's Rod* on. In *The First Lady Chatterley* (1926) it even seems to be the clue to further development. A passage about Soviet Russia as harsh as any in his work, from an essay of 1925, concludes, apropos of nothing: "But wait! There is life in the Russians. Something new and strange will emerge out of their weird transmogrification into Bolshevists" (*R* 117). Between 1926 and 1928, after his return from America, Lawrence was even planning a visit to Russia. He began learning the language and probably would have gone had he been less ill. But it was America's spirit of place that inspired his most intense prophetic effort.

Already in the early days of the war Lawrence was dreaming, like his Romantic predecessors, of getting away from Europe and founding a colony in the New World—perhaps in Florida, Texas, or the Southwest. As was his practice when about to venture to a new country, he undertook a study of its history and literature. The study was intensified after the suppression of *The Rainbow,* his most hard-won achievement, and under the growing strain of the war. During 1917 in Cornwall the first version of *Studies* was written.

In the opening essay, "The Spirit of Place," an uncanny exploration into the hidden will of historical movement, Lawrence speculates that, at about the time of the Renaissance, the polarity holding Italy-centered southern Europe and Germany-centered northern Europe had so weakened that the remoter regions of Spain, Holland, and England, already half under the spell of the Atlantic, became polarized with America and were thus impelled to discover it. The pull was felt from the other side as well, in American Indian legends about the white man arriving from beyond the sea. But the white man, adhering to Europe in his consciousness, overran the Indian without absorbing his spirit, which was the spirit of the continent itself. The prophetic historian finds America rich in promise, then, because it had not yet realized its spirit of place. Lack of tradition seemed to Lawrence— at least in 1920, before he came to America—an advantage; America could more easily slough off its European inheritance and fulfill its special destiny. The white consciousness in creative conjunction with the spirit of place was to lead us to a living religious idea. Lawrence set the challenge, of course, to the white man, for he was seeking a cultural development continuous with the one of which he was a part. The new must grow out of the old.

The actual history of American culture was "a false dawn," a divagation from its true goal. The Pilgrims' conscious intention in coming to America—religious liberty—was superficial, as was shown by the rigor of their laws; they really came in search of some positive fulfillment which liberty alone could not give. The profounder reason was twofold: a desire to escape the embryonic democratic idea of being masterless, which developed in the European psyche during the Renaissance; and a desire to find a new and vital idea of God. The evidence for this was to be found in the deepest expression of the American psyche, its art, which revealed in its "alien undertone" both a dissatisfaction with democracy and an effort to discover "the incipient realities" of a new era, i.e. a new God-idea consonant with the spirit of place.

But the actual experience of living in America clouded Lawrence's hope. The changes of detail made in the revisions of *Studies* interestingly reflect his disillusionment. In version I Benjamin Franklin's "extreme of conscious control" seemed a step toward psychic revolution. In version III it was simply mechanical idealism, not art-speech of any kind (*S* 35). Lawrence in Cornwall agreed with Crèvecoeur that it is easier for a white man to turn Indian than for an Indian to turn white. Lorenzo in Taos wrote, "I have seen some Indians whom you really couldn't tell from white men. And I have never seen a white man who looked really like an Indian. So Hector . . . is a liar" (*S* 43). In *Studies* I Lawrence scolded Cooper's wife for remarking that her husband glossed over the coarse actualities of the backwoods and for ignoring the myth-meaning of the novels. In *Studies* III he scolded Cooper himself for glossing over the coarse actualities. In 1917 the critic found that Natty Bumppo had gone beyond the old mode of consciousness to form a vital new comradeship with Chingachgook. In 1923 that meeting of white and Indian was "silent, reserved, across an unpassable distance."[9]

9. Armin Arnold deserves recognition for gathering *Studies* I and II into book form, but has rendered Lawrence no service in claiming them as the true text and categorically asserting that they have been "completely spoiled" in version III (*The Symbolic Meaning*, p. 6). True, they are less shrill and do contain some valuable material later omitted, but version III is superior in clarity, incisiveness, and force.

Having found the American spirit too taut and tense, the Australian too relaxed, and the Mexican "obsidian,"[1] Lawrence returned in 1925 to the Europe he had thought worn out and admitted that he had judged it too quickly. The European ease from which the Pilgrims had escaped was rechristened "insouciance" and "phallic glow," and was now preferable to the hardness of the American spirit. The depth of European tradition was perhaps an advantage after all, for "a place that is lived in lives" (P 117). But he would remain an outsider even in Europe. Like the hero of *The Boy in the Bush,* "he would return to civilization, but not to belong" (p. 241).

During the last years of his life Lawrence's interest in temporally remote civilizations increased, partly no doubt as a result of his disillusionment with the present. But it was still the sense of engagement with the present and of responsibility for the future that motivated him. Underlying all his evocations of a distant glamour is the sense of the urgency of present needs. Adherence to the actual is always the base of Lawrence's visionary flights.

T. S. Eliot has said that "the world was [Lawrence's] nightmare."[2] There is truth in this, and Lawrence, I imagine, must seem grotesque to many people of more moderate sensibilities. But one must qualify Eliot's remark by saying that, if Lawrence often hated where he was and what he was, it was always to this same time and place and to his own actual being that he would return. There was profound acceptance in him, too, of man's given nature and of the earth which is his home:

> For man the vast marvel is to be alive. For man, as for flower
> and beast and bird, the supreme triumph is to be most vividly
> alive. Whatever the unborn and the dead may know, they can-
> not know the beauty, the marvel of being alive in the flesh.
> The dead may look after the afterwards. But the magnificent
> here and now of life in the flesh is ours, and ours alone, and
> ours only for a time.   [*Apoc.* 199]

---

1. Neither Australia, which he visited before coming to America, nor Mexico, which he lived in during the latter part of his American sojourn, offered Lawrence much to build a psychic revolution upon. In *Kangaroo* and *The Plumed Serpent* the richly evoked spirit of place is more or less independent of the thought-adventure, the quest for a new mode of religious relationship.

2. Quoted in Tiverton, *Human Existence,* p. 98.

•┝━━━━━━━━━━━━━━━━━┥•

The intensity of Lawrence's desire for a better world has been responsible for two largely inaccurate impressions, which ought to be corrected for a proper understanding of the premises of his criticism: that he was a puritan moralist and that he was a critic of social forms and institutions.

Puritan moralism is perhaps present in some of his later journalism. In "Pornography and Obscenity," for example, he writes, "But even I would censor genuine pornography rigorously" (P 181). Yet this is misleading at best. Lawrence is everywhere so emphatic about the importance of confronting all dark desires and fears that by genuine pornography he must mean only the venal exploitation of a debased popular taste; and his scorn for such taste is usually humorous rather than solemn, when he stoops to it at all. His characteristic concern is a deeper one. The high-minded if unsuccessful use of obscene words in *Lady Chatterley's Lover* is essentially an effort to purify the *unconscious* by driving the fears attached to these words back up into the *mind,* where they can be dealt with for what they are instead of "returning upon us [from the unconscious], looming and magnified out of all proportion, frightening us beyond all reason" (*CP* 491).

Even Norman O. Brown, whose argument for the abolition of repression and the resurrection of the body reminds one of Lawrence, pegs Lawrence as the moral positivist who rejects Freud's Thanatos outright.[3] But only in a radical or ultimate sense did Lawrence—like Brown—believe the death wish to be not a product of human nature but of human culture. His constant effort was to confront and overcome it through greater self-consciousness. If we fail to realize this, we fall into the error of taking him to be a critic like F. R. Leavis, who is distrustful of those satirists in whom he does not find a clear assertion of positive value. Or we fall into the error of Edward McDonald, the editor of *Phoenix,* who wrote, "For him a book was good only if it revealed some original vision of life, some living, venturesome faith" (*P* xix). This is certainly a distortion of Lawrence's criticism, for his heroes of death are more numerous and important than his heroes of rebirth.

3. Norman O. Brown, *Life against Death* (New York, 1959), pp. 29, 181.

For the second misconception Lawrence is again partly responsible. He does appear at times the critic of social forms and institutions. But he was simply not interested enough in them to be regarded as a serious social critic. His solution to the "property question" was "to cease to be interested in it" (*CP* 665); as for money and machines, "Why have them? They belittle us" (*CP* 451–52). Nor, I think, did Lawrence regard himself as a serious social critic. "As a novelist, I feel that it is the change inside the individual which is my real concern. The great social change interests me and troubles me, but it is not my field" (*AA* 113). He made no real effort to implement his ideas through social action. "Writing is well enough as a means of action," he once told Middleton Murry. Sometimes he accepted his destiny grudgingly, but he did accept it. It is amusing to observe how he deals with an actual invitation to action. When Rolf Gardiner asked him to join his youth movement, the Kibbo Kift, Lawrence replied: "I should love to be connected with some few people, in something. As far as anything *matters,* I have always been very much alone, and regretted it. But I can't belong to clubs, or societies, or Freemasons, or any other damn thing. So if there is, with you, an activity I *can* belong to, I shall thank my stars. But, of course, I shall be wary beyond words, of committing myself" (*L* 667). This is almost too transparent to be called rationalization.

Yet in a more profound, psychological sense, art was emphatically a social activity and the artist a man who worked toward a more perfect social conception. Shakespeare in *Hamlet,* if he but knew it, was breaking down the old social conception based on the authority of King and Father (and heralding a new one based on fraternity) by suggesting conflicting duties toward it—an overstrained search for prophetic meaning only if we insist on the inviolability of conscious artistic intention.

Indeed, what most distinguishes Lawrence as a critic of culture is his acute perception of its unconscious predilections and prejudices, particularly as they inhibit the breadth and depth of an artist's vision. He understood well how popular art panders to our fear of exposing our fears and of changing our feelings, either by glorifying obsolescent social ideals or by titillating us with sin while preserving appearances. He knew well how feelings, under the pressure of cultural ideals, can become so polarized in our minds that even serious artists cannot get beyond good and evil and perceive value in the spontaneous currents of instinctual-imaginative life. Even the greatest, such as Milton in his picture of God, may rationalize, against their own instinct, their fear and hate of the instincts:

> That is the real pivot of bourgeois consciousness: fear and hate of the instincts. But of course this fear and hate had to take on a righteous appearance, so it became moral, said that the instincts were evil, and promised a *reward* for their suppression. That is the great clue to the bourgeois psychology: the reward business. Be good, and you'll have money. Be wicked, and you'll be utterly penniless at last, and the good ones will have to offer you a little charity. That is sound working morality in the world. And it makes one realize that, even to Milton, the true hero of *Paradise Lost* must be Satan."[4]   [*P* 559]

Perhaps the chief limitation of Lawrence's genuine social criticism, i.e. his psycho-social criticism, is its uncompromising high-mindedness. He attacked not only conscious but, especially, unconscious hypocrisy; he wanted not only moral behavior but moral feeling. Arguing from the questionable premise of radical innocence, he sought, as an ultimate goal, man purified of even the temptation to vice. He seemed to believe that vicious wishes, even when not fixated, were expungeable and that the instincts, free of mental interference, were inherently moral. It is here, I think, that Lawrence's thinking may truly be called puritanical. Getting down deep enough must really mean getting up high enough, where, by an immense effort of will (a will he supposed to be pre-reflective and attuned to the instrinsically purposive life thrust), the cruder forms of human aggression and sexuality could be utterly transformed into power and glory.

4. Lawrence shares with Blake and Shelley, then, the conviction that Milton's God is too paltry a conception to have represented the genuine belief of Milton the artist, however much Milton the man may have subscribed to him in his conscious mind. But his emphasis is a little different. Blake and Shelley put the emphasis on Satan's energy, which must have been drawn from Milton's deeper sympathy, though it is marred by his willed intention to show it as evil. Lawrence stresses the commonplaceness of Milton's God, His likeness to the middle-class morality of the last two hundred years.

7

The Case of Whitman and the Limits of Ideological Criticism

Ideological literary criticism, no matter how impressive in depth and breadth, is subject by its nature to fairly serious limitations. I shall try to define them in Lawrence's criticism by analyzing closely a particular case, and I have chosen for this purpose his study of Whitman, because it begins as a climax to his most sustained and important critical argument and ends smothered in its own excess.

Lawrence's procedure in *Studies in Classic American Literature* is based on two assumptions, which are both points of doctrine and inferences from the work at hand. The first is that the error of the white consciousness must be fully exposed, and was so exposed by the American classics, for he had discovered in them—as have more recent critics, notably Leslie Fiedler and Edward Dahlberg[1]—"a litany of white vice" (*S* 154). The second is that for rebirth to take place the white consciousness had to submit to creative conjunction with its opposite, "the spirit of place," and evidence for potential rebirth he thought he saw also in "the alien undertone" of these works. In his opening essay the critic declares his intention to discover the theme of rebirth as the synthesis of such a dialectic, but his occasional discovery of the theme in Cooper and Whitman is not as impressive as his discovery throughout of the stark exposure of the Puritan-

---

1. Leslie Fiedler, *Love and Death in the American Novel* (New York, 1960). Edward Dahlberg, *Can These Bones Live* (New York, 1960).

Democratic morality by the antithetical spirit of place: what Blake called "the consolidation of error." Thus "the maniacal fanaticism of the white mental consciousness" stands utterly revealed by Moby Dick, "the deepest blood being of the white race" (*S* 173). The implied promise of renewal may or may not be developed. The mere confrontation of the whalers by Moby Dick, like the stripping of Duessa by Arthur in Book I of *The Faerie Queene,* is a sufficient prophetic truth. Lawrence's reading of Whitman, like Yeats' vision of the Second Coming following "mere anarchy," is a development of the renewal latent in the consolidation of error.

Both of Lawrence's inferences are perceptions in depth. On the surface the Americans adhere to "the Love-and-produce cackle" (*S* 93). They "all feel uneasy about it. Sensuously, passionally, they all attack the old morality. But they know nothing better, mentally. Therefore they give tight mental allegiance to a morality which all their passion goes to destroy" (*S* 184). Since he finds little or no evidence that they are aware of their duplicity and so are ready to accept the responsibility for a new morality, he undertakes to read their tales against them, to save America from itself, to save it from democracy.

Lawrence's procedure is flexible enough to be fitted to individual authors. Crèvecoeur and Cooper scarcely suggest ideological tension; they reveal their dissatisfaction with the spiritual ideal only by presenting another knowledge in glimpses of animal life or in smooth fantasy. Poe, more bravely but more self-destructively, presses the old morality to the point of breakdown and insanity. Hawthorne is an almost conscious "satirist"—i.e. repudiator—who still clings gloatingly to sin: his duplicity is the most obvious: "His pious blame is a chuckle of praise all the while" (*S* 99). Melville reveals the mind's hatred of the blood with the profoundest sense of the demonic, but he sees only stark blankness as the result of this metaphysical warfare. Whitman contains both rhythms: he is the unconscious repudiator, and he is "the first white aboriginal," the first to fulfill the promise which originally lured the Pilgrims to America.

The essay on Whitman seems to make contradictory assertions in its two halves. It begins by asserting that Whitman's verses are "postmortem effects," the soul having died in *Moby Dick;* and it begins again after a midway break with the tribute, "Whitman, the great poet . . . the one man breaking a way ahead" (*S* 183). Actually, there is seeming contradiction even within the first half of the essay. The hilarious ridicule of Whitman's mechanical stridency in the opening pages gives way *before* the mid-point to the image of "a very great poet, of the end of life . . . of the transitions of the soul as it loses its integrity. The poet of the soul's last shout and shriek, on the confines of death" (*S* 182–83).

But all of this has its logic. Lawrence means, in the first half of the essay, that Whitman's ecstatic extremism has both a false and a true meaning. The false meaning is the poet's infatuation with Allness and One Direction, evident in the inflated rhetoric. The true meaning is established by reading Whitman's poetic development as if it were a tale, relating as cause and effect the ecstasy of oneness in *Song of Myself* to the death chants in *Calamus*. In the second half of the essay Lawrence discovers a second true meaning, a new doctrine of life. It is the deeper of the two truths. And it follows from the first as rebirth follows from a creative death, even though it is developed from another motif in the poetry.[2]

We must remind ourselves of the two meanings of death in Lawrence's metaphysical psychology. In the first pages of the essay death is understood as that egoistic nullity which is the penalty of adhering fixedly to an absolute, a special problem for the artist who seeks the extreme. But it gradually assumes a second meaning, the living death, the movement *into* which is necessary for creation. "Whitman would not have been the great poet he is if he had not taken the last steps and looked over into death," for "we have got to die in life, too, and disintegrate while we live" (*S* 183–84). Thinking of the soul *in extremis,* Lawrence, confusingly, speaks sometimes of the necessity for retraction and sometimes of the necessity for supercession. But in either case "the goal is not death. Something else will come" (*S* 184).[3] And in the second half of the essay Whitman, with Law-

2. Lawrence's method has confused Armin Arnold, who writes of this essay in *D. H. Lawrence and America,* "There is no unity in version 3. The second half is an attempt to improve on the severe judgment of Whitman in the first half" (p. 91).

3. T. S. Eliot is not correct in stating that Lawrence's belief in life "passed over into a belief in death, as a sincere belief in life must" (*After Strange Gods,* pp. 65–66). The truth is that for a writer with a sincere belief in life, like Lawrence, death must become a paramount issue.

rence's help, has taken the leap into new knowledge, breaking ground
and giving us a new doctrine of life.

The nature of Whitman's first, or "penultimate," truth is more
clearly explained in *Studies* II:

> Whitman has gone further, in actual living expression, than
> any man, it seems to me. Dostoevsky has burrowed underground
> into the decomposing psyche. But Whitman has gone forward
> in life-knowledge. It is he who surmounts the grand climacteric
> of our civilization.
>
> Whitman enters on the last phase of spiritual triumph. He
> really arrives at that stage of infinity which the seers sought.
> By subjecting the deepest *centres* of the lower self, he attains
> the maximum consciousness in the higher self; a degree of
> extensive consciousness greater, perhaps, than any man in the
> modern world.
>
> We have seen Dana and Melville, the two adventurers,
> setting out to conquer the last vast *element,* with the spirit. . . .
>
> Now we must remember that the way, even towards a state
> of infinite comprehension, is through the externals toward
> the quick. And the vast elements, the cosmos, the big things,
> the universals, these are always the externals. These are met
> and conquered first. That is why science is so much easier than
> art. The quick is the living being, and the quick of quicks is
> the individual soul. And it is here, at the quick, that Whitman
> proceeds to find the experience of infinitude, his vast extension,
> or concentrated intensification into Allness. He carries the con-
> quest to its end.   [*S* II, 232–33]

Lawrence is saying that the art of Melville and Whitman achieved
depth by instinctual apprehension rather than by self-conscious bur-
rowing, as did Dostoevsky's. But Whitman has gone farthest ("Melville
hunts the remote white whale of the deepest passional body, tracks it
down. But it is Whitman who captures the whale"), and is therefore
best equipped to envision the body's resurrection.

Before revealing the clue to rebirth, however, Lawrence must
instruct Whitman in the dangers of infinitude. He instructs him
first in what he calls, in a related essay, "the lesson of the fingers":
the truth that "the soul is never more than itself, though it embrace
eternity and infinity, and never more than itself, though it include
all men" (*P* 707). The second lesson is that the infinity of the spirit

is only a half truth; there is also a sensual infinity, an extreme of isolation rather than merging. And the movement toward one infinity without a sharp retraction to the other will overstrain the integral being so that it will "break . . . down like disintegrating tissue into slime, imbecility, epilepsy, vice, like Dostoevsky" (*S* II, 235).

Having explored Whitman's quest for infinitude, Lawrence is finally ready to reveal his ultimate truth, his clue to rebirth. In version II the clue is to be man-for-man love; in version III this is replaced by the idea of the isolate soul along the open road. In both, Lawrence interprets Whitman's poetry as a progressive movement in which the focus shifts from marriage to man-for-man love, the latter linked to death. In version II manly love still has creative possibility; in version III it has succumbed to dissolution, and a new possibility is found.

All of this, to be sure, sounds too little like Whitman and too much like Lawrence. It was Lawrence rather than Whitman who would make marriage the starting point for progressive development in relationship, and the critic must even admit that Whitman doesn't see woman properly, that his Female is only a biological unit in an abstract conception of democracy. Although both celebrate manly love, it was really Lawrence who associated it with death and who envisioned death as a creative matrix for a new era:

> The strange Calamus has its pink-tinged root by the pond, and it sends up its leaves of comradeship, comrades at one root, without the intervention of woman, the female. This comradeship is to be the final cohering principle of the new world, the new Democracy. It is the cohering principle of perfect soldiery, as [Whitman] tells us in "Drum Taps." It is the cohering principle of final *unison* in creative activity. And it is extreme and terrible to bear, terrible to be responsible for. It is the soul's last and most vivid responsibility, the responsibility for the circuit of final friendship, comradeship, manly love.

Lawrence here, in version II, is straining to make Whitman his prophetic forerunner. But he adds ingenuously: "The last phase is entered upon, shakily, by Whitman. It will take us an epoch to establish the new, perfect circuit of our being."

A few years later, disillusioned in comrade-love as a result of his stormy relationship with Middleton Murry, and disillusioned also, it seems, with America as a result of having lived in it, Lawrence himself enters shakily upon this last phase:

> Over and over he says the same thing: the new world will be built on the love of comrades, the new great dynamic of life will be manly love. Out of this manly love will come the inspiration for the future.
> Will it though? Will it?
> Comradeship! Comrades! This is to be the new Democracy: of Comrades. . . .
> Is it? Are you sure? . . .
> There you have the progression of merging. For the great mergers, woman at last becomes inadequate. For those who love to extremes. Woman is inadequate for the last merging. So the next step is the merging of man-for-man love. And this is on the brink of death. It slides over into death.
> David and Jonathan. And the death of Jonathan.
> It always slides into death. . . .   [S 180–82]

For David and Jonathan I'm afraid we are to read David Herbert Lawrence and John Middleton Murry.

If the love of comrades has become by 1923 an obsolete ideal and if Lawrence still wants to find a new vision of life in Whitman, he must develop it from a new motif in the work. And this is what he does in the latter half of version III:

> Whitman was the first to break the mental allegiance. He was the first to smash the old moral conception, that the soul of man is something "superior" and "above" the flesh. . . .
> "There!" he said to the soul. "Stay there!"
> Stay there. Stay in the flesh. Stay in the limbs and lips and in the belly.
>   . . .
> The Open Road. The great home of the soul is the open road. Not heaven, not paradise. Not "above." Not even "within." The soul is neither "above" nor "within." It is a wayfarer down the open road. . . .
> Not through charity. Not through sacrifice. Not even through love. Not through good works. Not through these does the soul accomplish herself.

Only through the journey down the open road. . . . Exposed to full contact. On two slow feet. . . . Towards no goal. Always the open road.

Having no known direction, even. Only the soul remaining true to herself in her going.

Meeting all the other wayfarers along the road. And how? How meet them, and how pass? With sympathy, says Whitman. Sympathy. He does not say love. He says sympathy. Feeling with. Feel with them as they feel with themselves. Catching the vibration of their soul as we pass.

It is a new great doctrine of life. A new great morality. A morality of actual living, not of salvation. . . .

It is not I who guide my soul to heaven. It is I who am guided by my own soul along the open road, where all mean tread. Therefore I must accept her deep motions of love, or hate, or compassion, or dislike, or indifference. And I must go where she takes me. . . .

This is Whitman's message of American democracy.

The true democracy, where soul meets soul, in the open road. . . . And where a soul is known at once in its going. . . . And recognized, and passed by, or greeted according to the soul's dictate. [*S* 184–90]

It is amusing to discover that Whitman's new doctrine consists of those very ideas which were earlier thought to be violated in his art: that the soul is and should be inseparable from the body and that true sympathy means maintaining distance at least as much as merging. And in order to read the tale against the artist, almost a pretense by now, Lawrence must translate some of Whitman's key terms: democracy, sympathy, and personality.

In related essays Lawrence wrote that "Whitman was almost conscious, only the political democracy issue confused him" (*P* 91) and that the elements of democracy for Whitman were the Average, Identity, and Personality (*P* 710). The Average must be rejected, for "the only riches [are] the great souls" in an ideal democracy. Identity insofar as it means merging into Allness must also go because it precludes otherness, but insofar as it means Love, and Love means Sympathy, and Sympathy means living according to the soul's dictate, it is all right; but it must not be confused with "Jesus' LOVE and

139

with Paul's CHARITY" (*S* 186). And Personality is false because it is an expression of the ego; the truer term is Individuality (*P* 710).[4]

Although Lawrence is, on the whole, harsher with Whitman—and with all the Americans—in version III than he was in version II, his proclamation of Whitman's true doctrine is more exuberant, probably because it consisted of those general principles in which he never lost faith: the centrality of selfhood and the openness of life. Yet at the end of the essay, which is also the end of the book, Lawrence cannot refrain from offering, if only tentatively, a more concrete possibility to be explored. It is the leader and follower theme, the "clue" which the critic was at the time exploring in his art. Thus he concludes:

> A glad recognition of souls, and a gladder worship of great and greater souls, because they are the only riches.
> Love and Merging brought Whitman to the Edge of Death! Death! Death!
> But the exultance of his message still remains. Purified of MERGING, purified of MYSELF, the exultant message of American Democracy, of souls in the Open Road, full of fierce readiness, full of joy of worship, when one soul sees a greater soul.
> The only riches, the great souls.   [*S* 191]

This idea is not from Whitman, nor does Lawrence pretend to look for it there. It is a kind of coda, the purpose of which, like the purpose of many concluding passages in Lawrence, is not so much to sum up the work in hand as to look forward to the work that will follow.

·┤——————————————├·

There are broadly speaking two approaches to literary values: the ideological or moral and the formal or aesthetic. As a rule, the first is more successfully carried out by men of letters, the second by scholars. The criteria of effectiveness are basically the same for both: force and intelligence, and by intelligence I mean perception and relevance. But force and intelligence tend to take different forms in

---

4. Individuality for Personality may actually be a legitimate translation, a closer approximation of the sense of Whitman's word than the modern word personality.

the two cases. The force of moral criticism is usually more personal, deriving to a greater extent from the intensity and scope of the critic's view of life. The force of formal criticism is usually more impersonal, deriving to a greater extent from the manner in which evidence is organized and presented. Failure of intelligence in moral criticism is likely to emerge as extravagance. Failure of intelligence in formal criticism is likely to emerge as dullness.

The difficulties apparent in Lawrence's essays on Whitman are not a result of his being personal. His literary criticism on the whole is remarkable for the degree to which personal beliefs *merge* with perceptive and relevant commentary, and there can, I think, be no legitimate charge against subjective literary criticism as long as it is sufficiently objective at the same time. (Coleridge on Hamlet—*pace* Eliot—is *not* bad criticism. It is quite sufficiently perceptive and relevant. It is not the whole truth about Hamlet, but then nothing is.) Nor do Lawrence's essays on Whitman lack interest. But there is some failure of intelligence—a lack of relevance, I should say, rather than of perception. They are interesting in a way, but one keeps feeling that they should be either more or less about Whitman.

There seem to be two Lawrencean ideas, the supercession of marriage by manly love and the diabolism of modern woman, which are particularly likely to deflect his critical intelligence, although they are sometimes successfully drawn forth from the work at hand. The first idea is fairly successfully drawn from Cooper, not so successfully from Whitman. The second is quite successfully revealed in the essays on Poe, but not in *The Scarlet Letter:* it prompts the critic to discuss for pages the reasons behind the Hester-Dimmesdale seduction, a concern not relevant to the novel itself. As for the occasional disingenuous irrelevancies, such as the David and Jonathan remark, they may be explained as either willful self-indulgence or compulsive self-expression, depending on one's sympathy for the kind of person Lawrence was.

Lack of perception is most apparent when his interest is not aroused, or when impatience prevents him from discovering his interest. His comments on Proust and Joyce are illustrative:

> "Did I feel a twinge in my little toe, or didn't I?" asks every
> character of Mr. Joyce or of Miss Richardson or of M. Proust.

Is my aura a blend of frankincense and orange pekoe and
boot-blacking, or is it myrrh and bacon-fat and Shetland tweed?
The audience round the death-bed gapes for the answer. And
when, in a sepulchral tone, the answer comes at length, after
hundreds of pages: "It is none of these, it is abysmal chloro-
coryambasis," the audience quivers all over, and murmurs:
"That's just how I feel myself."

Which is the dismal, long-drawn-out comedy of the death-
bed of the serious novel. It is self-consciousness picked into
such fine bits that the bits are most of them invisible, and you
have to go by the smell. Through thousands and thousands of
pages Mr. Joyce and Miss Richardson tear themselves to pieces,
strip their smallest emotions to the finest threads, till you feel
you are sewed inside a wool mattress that is being slowly
shaken up, and you are turning to wool along with the rest of
the woolliness.   [*P* 517–18]

Comic exaggeration aside, these remarks are not so much wrong-
headed as commonplace. Lawrence perceives in Joyce and Proust the
extreme self-consciousness that any critic would perceive, and he has
little to add but the force of his disapproval. That disapproval is
wittily expressed and inevitably has the tangential interest of further
delineating his own rich sensibility, but it does not add much to our
sense of Joyce and Proust.

Lawrence is the kind of critic whose need is to reveal rather than
point out, and who is therefore best when he is excited enough to
work in depth. Thus engaged, he ignores completely the whiteness of
Melville's whale, the role of the narrator in Poe's "Ligeia," or the
surface resemblances between Whitman's ideas and his own. Such
a need may seem more temperamental than intellectual, but I think
it is to be expected in any penetrating criticism that is less concerned
with language and structure than with states of mind and ideology.[5]

In any case, this ability to reveal, this gift for detecting psychological

5. Lawrence's interest in ideology may partly explain his difficulty with
Whitman and with lyrical verse generally. In the absence of a narrative, the
critic comes down too hard on particular themes and phrases. He wrote in
"Democracy": "In Whitman, at all times, the true and false are so near, so
interchangeable, that we are almost inevitably left with divided feelings"
(*P* 709)—a comment that makes less sense as a report on Whitman than as a
report on Lawrence's difficulty with Whitman.

undercurrents and hidden biases, is Lawrence's chief distinction as a literary critic. His comments on the diabolical undertone in classic American fiction, on the every-man-his-own hero theme in Dostoevsky, on the conscious reverence but unconscious contempt for women in the English novel in contrast to the conscious contempt but unconscious reverence for them in Greek drama—this kind of insight, abundant in his work, is very impressive. The limitations of ideological criticism begin to be evident when the prophetic Lawrence patterns his insight into a grand view. Many perceptions are achieved in the process, and the synthesis itself is, in a way, impressive, but the increasing uniformity makes for predictability and monotony, and offends against our experience of amplitude, density, and variety.[6] And when the prophetic Lawrence becomes the Messianic Lawrence, when he is not content to discover in serious modern art unwelcome tendencies but must dismiss it as utterly exhausted, then relevance and perception are so drastically reduced that he has ceased to function effectively as a literary critic.

These three perspectives—the psychological, the prophetic, and the Messianic—are successively apparent in the essay on Whitman and account for its decreasing effectiveness. Let me illustrate the sequence in another context in order to make the point as clearly as possible.

We remember in "The Novel" that Lawrence approached *Anna Karenina* from the assumption that all genuine artists—and therefore Tolstoi—are in their deepest selves "phallic worshippers." This seems at first a Lawrencean idea imposed on Tolstoi, and Lawrence makes clear that Tolstoi the Man—Leo—did not share it. But it is precisely this conflict between artist and man *in the book* that Lawrence succeeds in showing us. Tolstoi does project a strong current of sympathy for Anna in her struggle with society—and seems to acknowledge it in his chosen epigraph, "Vengeance is mine; I will repay, saith the Lord"— but he also conveys, especially in the later chapters, a distinct coldness toward her, as if he is taking vengeance into his own hands. It is this Tolstoi who later berated himself for writing about something as

6. The prophetic Lawrence tends to interpret art and historical, nonartistic structures in about the same way. World War I "reads" like *The Scarlet Letter:* it was sensational delight masked as pious idealism. Psychoanalysis "reads" like Poe or Dostoevsky: it was disintegrative activity, valuable in exposing dead ideals but not able to lead us to new life.

trivial as a married woman's affair with an officer. A moral assumption is thus *absorbed* by the implications of the work being discussed.

But Lawrence's prophetic earnestness prompts him to carry his attack one step further: Tolstoi, along with Dostoevsky and Chekhov, is to be blamed for the coming on of Bolshevism:

> One cannot now help thinking
> how much better it would have been
> if Vronsky and Anna Karenin
> had stood up for themselves, and seen
> Russia across her crisis,
> instead of leaving it to Lenin.
>
> The big, flamboyant Russia
> might have been saved, if a pair
> of rebels like Anna and Vronsky
> had blasted the sickly air
> of Dostoevsky and Tchekov,
> and spy-government everywhere.
>
> But Tolstoi was a traitor
> to the Russia that needed him most,
> the clumsy, bewildered Russia
> so worried by the Holy Ghost.
> He shifted his job on to the peasants
> and landed them all on toast.
>
> Dostoevsky, the Judas,
> with his sham christianity
> epileptically ruined
> the last bit of sanity
> left in the hefty bodies
> of the Russian nobility.
>
> So our goody-good men betray us
> and our sainty-saints let us down,
> and a sickly people will slay us
> if we touch the sob-stuff crown
> of such martyrs; while Marxian tenets
> naturally take hold of the town.
>
> Too much of the humble Willy wet-leg
> and the holy can't-help-it-touch,
> till you've ruined a nation's fibre

and they loathe all feeling as such,
and want to be cold and devilish hard
like machines—and you can't wonder much.—

[CP 536-37]

There is enough force, perception, and relevance here to hold our interest, but there is also a leveling out of literary values: three great writers are presented almost indistinguishably, and the relation between art and historical process is much oversimplified.

The third step is the moralistic obliteration of aesthetic judgment, the simple rejection of antipathetic artistic objectives:

The cells of Tchekov's writing [are] disintegrating cells, emitting, as they burst, a doleful twang which remains with us.

[CB 3, 13]

My God, what a clumsy *olla putrida* James Joyce is! Nothing but old fags and cabbage-stumps of quotations from the Bible and the rest, stewed in the juice of deliberate, journalistic dirty-mindedness—what old and hard-worked staleness, masquerading as the all-new! [L 742]

This is, I am sure, impatience rather than insensitivity, but it comes to the same thing.

8

Conclusion

[Criticism's] greatest single attribute is its force, its passionate declaration of the true nature of man and what his proper destiny must be. . . . The greatest examples of such criticism in modern times were Arnold's essays on poetry and culture, Proust's attack on Sainte-Beuve, and Nietzsche's on Wagner. To me this is the most valuable kind of criticism—the kind that Baudelaire wrote in dealing with art, Shaw in dealing with drama, and that before them had been practiced by Goethe in his remarks on the Age of Prose, by Schiller in his letters on aesthetics, by Blake in his personal manifestoes, by Wordsworth in his preface to *Lyrical Ballads.* It is the kind of criticism I always think of as *histoire morale,* that sums up the spirit of the age in which we live and then asks us to transcend it, that enables us to see things in the grand perspective, and that in the way of Marx on Greek philosophy, of Kierkegaard on Mozart, of Nietzsche on the birth of tragedy, of Shaw on Ibsen, of Lawrence on American literature, asks us—not only in the light of man's history but of his whole striving—to create a future in keeping with man's imagination. . . .

Criticism, in our modern sense of it . . . has led to an awareness of aesthetic possibilities and of individual vision which unites *all* modern poets, novelists, painters, whether they acknowledge it or not, as children of the Romantic movement. The point of this modern spirit in art is not that everyone agrees on the value of the modern movement, but that everyone must work in its atmosphere of freedom and individual discovery. . . .

Conclusion

The critic who has the equipment to be a force, the critic who can set up standards for his age, must be a partisan of one kind of art and a bitter critic of another. . . . Such a critic will be not only unfair, he will pursue his prejudice to the point of absurdity, setting up a straw figure that will serve to bear all his dislike and even his hatred of a certain kind of art. . . . Above all, the critic who works with this sense of the age in his bones, who sees himself working toward the future that man must build for himself, is always a writer. He writes for the public, not to a few imagined co-specialists; he writes to convince, to argue, to establish an argument; he writes dramatically, marshaling his evidence in a way that pure logic would never approve and pure scholarship would never understand, but which is justifiable, if it succeeds, as moral argument in the great tradition of literature.[1]

[Lawrence as critic] participates in an odd kind of subtradition of his own made up of intellectual renegades, of violently creative minds, of brilliant and angry men whom the ordering techniques of the historian never quite succeed in assimilating into the homogeneous textures of their "periods."

One thinks of Dante, of Milton, of Swift, of Voltaire, perhaps of Thoreau, and even of Dr. Johnson; and in our time, certainly of Gide, of Shaw, of Pound. It isn't sufficient simply to label such men "iconoclasts," for they are makers as well as breakers. They are indeed "originals," and they are that long after they have become part of cultural history; but they are toughly men of intellect also, and so one does not think of Shelley with these. They possess compulsively responsive moral natures that must be expressed: thus the sharp and special "insights" they seem to have while most of their contemporaries, small and great, go on confirming the historical process. Such men never achieve revolutions—*make* history—though they make disciples as readily as they make enemies. They are too selfish and inconsistent to lead causes. They are never specialists, always instinctively amateurs. And their prejudices are queer, pronounced, grotesque, sometimes verging upon the insane.[2]

1. Alfred Kazin, "The Function of Criticism Today," *Commentary*, 30, No. 5 (1960), 370–73.
2. Richard Foster, "Criticism as Rage," in Moore, *Miscellany*, pp. 312–13.

Lawrence's basic procedure as a literary critic is to bring his vision of the nature and destiny of man into meaningful relation with works of literary art. Such a procedure may be called subjective or personal, but only in a restricted sense. Lawrence has so fully identified himself with his doctrine that, despite the obvious personal reference of his work and despite the fact that we possess so much biographical information about him, explanation and interpretation by way of biography become to a large extent superfluous.

Lawrence takes for granted that his experience is representative. It is an assumption that works, because his consciousness was acutely sensitive to a real, objective world. William York Tindall scoffs at Lawrence's "fashionable mind,"[3] but it was his very responsiveness to the spirit of the age that enabled Lawrence to speak to us, for all his prejudices, about a common experience. Blackmur remarks, "As it happens, Lawrence's obsessions ran to sex, death, the isolation of the personality, and the attempt at mystical fusion. Had he run rather to claustrophobia, fetish-worship, or some of the more obscure forms of human cowardice, his method of expression would have been less satisfactory: since it would not have commanded the incipient hysteria of sympathy."[4] This seems to me the *reductio* of the Hulmean idea that subject matter is not important. Lawrence didn't just happen to be interested in important subjects; it is precisely in the intuitive sense of what is essentially important to one's age, and of what is fundamental in any age, that a large measure of creative or critical intelligence lies.

We must insist on Lawrence's intelligence over Eliot's objection and, in a way, over his own. He had little sense of detachment but profound self-awareness. His objective and subjective awareness were almost one, so that every venture into criticism was both a perception of a real, objective world and an exercise in self-knowledge. What is remarkable in Lawrence is not that he was sometimes wrested from his grip on his critical subject by the counterforce of some personal obsession but that his criticism so often combined force *with* relevance.

Lawrence was able to subordinate art to life and still write effective criticism, because his concept of life included, or was identified with,

3. *D. H. Lawrence and Susan His Cow*, p. 59.
4. *Form and Value*, p. 264.

a serious and workable concept of art. His "life" signified botl
and "ought"; it was both descriptive and honorific; the critic's wo
distinctions were between life and nonlife rather than betwee
and art. He did not really deny that art is an autonomous stru
symbolically related to life; he simply very often succeeded in me
moral and aesthetic judgment.

But this is an obviously risky procedure for literary criticisr
one thing, it puts pressure (sometimes lethal) on the formal int
of works of art, not to speak of the integrity of genres. For ar
it means that when art and life cannot be brought into se
relation, there is likely to be a failure of perception or relevanc
thirdly, as Lawrence's practice makes quite clear, because it
vigorous and uncompromising, there is a serious limitation in
in any criticism from a definite position: the exclusion of
possible points of view, which means very often the abrupt di
of kinds of art for which the critic has little or no tolerance
did make a nearly dreadful mistake glorifying those business
in *Howard's End*," he wrote to E. M. Forster. "Business is no
(*L* 552). The "nearly" can only be courtesy.

Much depends then on the scope, intrinsic interest, and con
rary relevance of the doctrine itself. The first two by now shou
been amply demonstrated. Contemporary relevance is a more
tain matter, but if there is a significant degree of truth in
opinion that we are all children of the Romantic movemen
perhaps it can be affirmed. For the central tenets of Romanti
—the authority of the individual and what Kazin calls "the
tion of life by the imagination"—are also central tenets in Law

I think Kazin and Foster, as well as Turnell, whom I qu
earlier chapters, have given us good accounts of the effect
especially the force, of Lawrence's kind of criticism. It seem
they have muffled most opposition by granting what need
granted, particularly the violent prejudices characteristic of
moral criticism. Others have mentioned Lawrence's nearness to
without knowing what to make of it. His *nearness* to hyste
measure not of his loose grip on reality but, on the contrar

5. There seems to be broadening agreement on this point. The ess;
recent *A D. H. Lawrence Miscellany*, for example, though selected for
evince a fairly consistent theme: Lawrence and the Romantic moven

intense engagement with reality. One criterion of moral greatness is surely the degree to which a man can take reality into consciousness without losing hold.[6] Far from thinking Lawrence volatile or weak-minded, I can only marvel at the fundamental strength of mind that enabled him to maintain such acute awareness while carrying his desire to extremes.

Kazin and Foster are right, I think, in placing Lawrence in an eclectic tradition composed of many of the most forceful and independent men of letters in the last two hundred years. Eliot himself helped to explain why such men are often great critics when he wrote in *The Sacred Wood,* "The two directions of sensibility [the creative and the critical] are complementary, and as sensibility is rare, unpopular and desirable, it is to be expected that the critic and the creative artist should frequently be the same person."[7] Eliot, of course, would be reluctant to admit that uncompromising trust in private judgment gives Lawrence any of his moral authority. But the authority of Eliot's antagonism is considerably weakened when we realize—as many are now coming to do—that he and critics of his school are also, but covertly, ideological.

There is one point, however, which Kazin, Foster, and Turnell do not make sufficiently clear. If the school of Eliot is prejudiced in favor of formal criticism, they, I think, are prejudiced against it. They tend to regard moral force as the standard for all good criticism and to ignore the strength of good formal criticism. In this they are perhaps more Romantic than they know: they would all be "originals."

Perhaps the best defense of formal against ideological criticism comes not from an Eliotian critic but from Northrop Frye. Stating a basic principle for a sound formal criticism, Frye writes, "One's 'definite position' is one's weakness, the source of one's liability to error and prejudice."[8] Frye is keenly aware of how much modern criticism is, at bottom, moral argument and therefore subject to the changing history of taste; his objective, accordingly, is to re-establish the basis for something like a scientific criticism.

Apparently Frye would have little use for Lawrence as a critic.

6. It is more or less on this basis, in fact, that Richard Rees has argued for a view of Lawrence as "a natural saint." See his *Brave Men,* pp. 36 ff.

7. T. S. Eliot, *The Sacred Wood* (London, 1945), p. 16.

8. *Anatomy of Criticism,* p. 19.

Conclusion

But in the final chapter of his *Anatomy of Criticism* he directs us to an important source of the strength which Lawrence brought to criticism. "We soon realize," he writes, "that the only really consistent moral criticism . . . would be the kind which is harnessed to an all-round revolutionary philosophy of society, such as we find not only in Marxism but in Nietzsche and in some of the rationalizations of oligarchic values in nineteenth-century Britain and twentieth-century America."[9] This kind of frank and all-round revolutionary philosophy is exactly what we find in Lawrence. And it clearly makes possible, in the hands of a skilled practitioner, a penetrating, if inevitably limited, criticism of literature.

The gain is worth the loss. After all, we are profoundly and naturally interested in moral values. Moreover, critics who bring moral values to bear upon literature with enough force and intelligence can to some extent survive the mutations of taste. The taste of Johnson and Arnold is no longer ours, but their criticism, being a kind of art, still lives.

In conclusion, I shall, in the briefest way, try to account for the obvious and widespread interest in Lawrence during the last two decades.

It is a little puzzling, despite what I have said. I would find it hard to disagree with Middleton Murry's statement, written shortly before his death in 1957, "[Lawrence's] significance itself is no longer in debate. Yet as poet and novelist he has no imitators; as prophet no successors. . . . The figure whom he chiefly calls to my mind is Rousseau, but whereas Rousseau opened an epoch, Lawrence seems to have closed one."[1] A few imitators and successors could perhaps be found—Henry Miller, Tennessee Williams, Norman Mailer, Wright Morris—but to name them does more to strengthen Murry's point than to weaken it. Lawrence does seem to be the last Romantic, the last of those radical individualists who set themselves against an entire culture and still stood for something meaningful. Since his death, the rapidly increasing power of the state and of mass-organization have made such tremendous assertions of selfhood all but impossible.

9. Ibid., p. 346.
1. Middleton Murry, "D. H. Lawrence: Creative Iconoclast," in Moore, *Miscellany,* pp. 3–4.

Chapter Eight

It may then be nostalgia which sends so many scholars and general readers back to Lawrence, nostalgia for an heroic conception of man and society, for a belief in radical innocence and in an infinitely open future. But I believe there is something profounder involved in our interest too, something that makes Romanticism not just the name for a period of history but also for some permanent stratum of thought and feeling. For, through all the shifts of ideology, through all the doctrines that men have lived by during the past two hundred years, persists the Romantic knowledge that the mind of man is sole author and creator of human culture. A man who passionately believes that "Destiny lies in the strength of our desires" (*CL* 344), and who is at the same time intelligent enough to understand that "no man is great enough to rise clean above his times" (*P* 748), must appear to us as a hero. Our faith in self-transcendence may have receded, but it cannot have disappeared.

Appendix

An Index to Lawrence's Literary Criticism

Listed here are the names of authors on whom Lawrence made significant comment and the places where his comments are to be found. The following abbreviations are used:

AA	*Assorted Articles*
Apoc.	*Apocalypse*
"A Propos"	"A Propos of Lady Chatterley's Lover"
CB	*D. H. Lawrence: A Composite Biography*
CL	*The Collected Letters of D. H. Lawrence*
CP	*The Complete Poems of D. H. Lawrence*
F	*Fantasia of the Unconscious*
L	*The Letters of D. H. Lawrence*
P	*Phoenix: The Posthumous Papers of D. H. Lawrence*
R	*Reflections on the Death of a Porcupine and Other Essays*
S	*Studies in Classic American Literature*
SL	*The Selected Letters of D. H. Lawrence*
SLC	*D. H. Lawrence: Selected Literary Criticism*
SM	*The Symbolic Meaning: The Uncollected Versions of Studies in Classic American Literature*

Full publication information is provided in the Bibliography.

Abercrombie	*CL* 253, 278; *P* 305
Aeschylus	*CL* 326; *P* 439, 476–77, 481–82, 512, 514, 551; *Twilight in Italy* 94–95
Anderson, Sherwood	*CL* 599; *P* 272
Apuleius	*SM* 16–17
Aretino	*CL* 1050

Appendix

Aristophanes	P 170
Austen	"A Propos" 119; P 540
Balzac	CL 35–36, 39–40, 43; SM 231
Baring, Maurice	P 386
Baudelaire	SM 231–32
Belloc	SLC 138
Bennett	CL 150, 1049
The Bible	Apoc. passim; P 292–303, 535–36; SL 86–89; SM 69, 213; R 107–10; The Boy in the Bush 246
Blake	P 560; Chambers, D. H. Lawrence: A Personal Record 62; Brewster, D. H. Lawrence: Reminiscences and Correspondence 86 (see below, Bib.)
Boccaccio	P 174–77, 274–76
Bottomley, Gordon	P 306
Brontë, Charlotte	P 174–77, 337, 562
Brontë, Emily	P 225–26
Brooke, Rupert	P 305
Browning	L 853
Bunyan	P 295
Burns	CL 169; P 180, 182; SLC 52
Byron	P 322, 459
Casanova	SLC 254
Chaucer	P 551–52
Chekhov	CB 3 13; CP 533–34, 536–37; P 223, 227–28; SLC 242
Colette	CL 213
Conrad	CL 152, 527; R 108; S 142; SM 199; Carswell, Savage Pilgrimage 197 (see below, Bib.)
Cooper	CL 488; S 43–73, 122; SM 68–81, 85–103, 213
Crèvecoeur	S 31–43; SM 50–66, 213
Crosby, Harry	P 257–62
Dahlberg, Edward	CL 1108–09; P 267–73
Dana	CL 454; S 121–42; SM 159, 213
D'Annunzio	CL 488; SL 86; P 224, 243, 263, 276
Dante	CP 711, 714; R 115–16

Davies	*CL* 47, 236
Dekker, E. D.	*P* 236–39
De La Mare	*P* 306
Deledda, Grazia	*P* 263–66
De Quincey	*L* 484; *SM* 119–20, 142–43
Dickens	*CB* 3 23, 581; *CL* 226; *P* 324, 493, 540; *SM* 231
Doolittle, Hilda	Bynner, *Journey with Genius* 145 (see below, Bib.)
Donne	*P* 552
Dos Passos	*P* 270, 363–65
Dostoevsky	*CB* 3 293; *CL* 53–54, 281–82, 420, 429–32, 492; *CP* 533–34, 536–37; *L* 180; *P* 227–28, 238, 283–91, 367–71, 390, 512, 530; *R* 55–60; *S* 12; *SLC* 229, 232, 242; *SM* 56, 80, 232; Murry, *Reminscences of D. H. Lawrence* 81–85 (see below, Bib.)
Dreiser	*P* 272
Edgeworth, Maria	*P* 559
Eliot, George	*CL* 34, 42; *P* 224, 562; Chambers, *D. H. Lawrence: A Personal Record* 97–98, 105 (see below, Bib.)
Eliot, T. S.	*SLC* 21
Emerson	*P* 316–17
Euripides	*CL* 76; *P* 477, 514
Fielding	"A Propos" 119; *P* 493, 552
Flaubert	*P* 226–27, 304, 312–13; *S* 189; *The Noble Savage* 2 248 (see below, Bib.)
Flecker, James Elroy	*CL* 244; *L* 135
Forster	*CL* 799, 800; *L* 552, 615
France, Anatole	*CL* 827; *R* 108
Franklin	*P* 316; *S* 19–31; *SM* 34–47, 50–51, 213
Galsworthy	*P* 540–50, 763; *Touch and Go* 8–12; Tedlock, *D. H. Lawrence Manuscripts* 170 (see below, Bib.)
Garnett, David	*CL* 800; *SLC* 140
Garnett, Edward	*L* 84
Gibson, W. W.	*CL* 253; *P* 305

Gide	*CL* 991; *P* 270
Gissing	*CL* 47, 94
Goethe	*AA* 155; *CL* 1049; *P* 131, 309
Gray, Thomas	*P* 323
Grazzini, A. F. (Lasca)	*P* 274–78
Hardy	*CL* 488, 1069; *CP* 873–74; *P* 304, 410–21, 434–40, 480–510; *S* 71, 101, 122; *SM* 99–100, 231–32
Hawthorne	*CL* 584; *P* 318–19; *S* 12, 92–121; *SM* 122–46, 148–58, 213
Hecht, Ben	*CL* 725–26
Heine	*P* 180
Hemingway	*P* 365–66
Herodotus	*SM* 59
Hodgson	*CL* 236–37
Homer	*CL* 326; *P* 218, 228–29; *SM* 86, 90
Housman	*CL* 44
Hugo	*P* 247–48
Huxley, Aldous	*CL* 1019–20, 1096, 1123; *P* 270
Ibsen	*CL* 152, 174; *P* 304
James, Henry	*CL* 388
Joyce	*CL* 1075–76, 1087; *P* 250, 270, 517–18; *R* 108; Brett, *Lawrence and Brett: A Friendship* 81 (see below, Bib.)
Keats	*AA* 155; *P* 40–44, 560–61
Lewis, Sinclair	*P* 519; *R* 108
Lowell, Amy	*SL* 143–44
Macaulay	*P* 539
Maeterlinck	*SM* 231–32
Mallarmé	*P* 512; *SM* 231–32
Mann	*P* 308–13; *SL* 86
Mansfield	*CB* 2 410; *CL* 488, 759; Carswell, *The Savage Pilgrimage* 198 (see below, Bib.)
Manzoni	*P* 223
Masefield	*CL* 191; *P* 305–06
Masters	*CL* 413
Maugham	*CL* 816; *P* 386–87
Maupassant	*F* 138

Melville   *CL* 454; *S* 142–74; *SM* 199–209, 211–28, 232, 235
Meredith   *P* 540
Merimee   *F* 220; *P* 248
Miller, Joaquin   *P* 320
Milton   *P* 559
Pater   *P* 539
Petronius   *CL* 420
Poe   *P* 334–36; *R* 59; *S* 73–92; *SM* 106–20, 213
Pope   *P* 719–20
Proust   *CP* 533–34; *P* 517–18; *Lady Chatterley's Lover* chap. 13

Richardson, Dorothy   *P* 517–18
Richardson, Samuel   *P* 174–77, 552
Rolfe, Frederick   *P* 327–30
Rousseau   *P* 750–51; *SM* 39–40, 50–51
Rozanov   *P* 367–71, 388–92
Rutherford, Mark   *L* 80–81; *SLC* 138
Sainte-Beuve   *P* 539
Sandburg   *P* 320
Shakespeare   *AA* 155; *CB* 3 13; *CP* 494, 508; *P* 170, 180, 227, 256, 309, 313, 420, 439–40, 513, 536, 541, 543, 551, 555; *S* 109; *SL* 5; *Twilight in Italy* 93–102; Chambers, *D. H. Lawrence: A Personal Record* 59 (see below, Bib.); Murry, *Reminiscences* 65 (see below, Bib.)
Shaw   "A Propos" 100–02; *CL* 12, 42, 44, 877, 1069; *F* 149; *SLC* 132
Shelley   *CL* 244, 253, 474; *P* 459, 478, 560; *SM* 50–51
Shestov   *P* 215–17
Sophocles   *CL* 76; *P* 420, 439, 541, 551
Spenser   *Apoc.* 8
Stendahl   *CL* 94, 860, 1085; *The Noble Savage* 2 248 (see below, Bib.)
Stephens, James   *CL* 250
Strindberg   *CL* 152, 169
Swift   "A Propos" 94; *CP* 419–20; *P* 281–82, 552
Swinburne   *CL* 454, 474; *P* 478, 552; *S* 142

Synge	*CL* 76; *SLC* 132
Theocritus	*P* 243
Thoreau	*S* 122
Thucydides	*CL* 454
Tolstoi	*CB* 3 13; *CL* 54, 250, 281–82; *CP* 533–34, 536–37; *F* 220–21; *P* 246, 391, 420, 479; *R* 104–23; *SLC* 242; Chambers, *D. H. Lawrence: A Personal Record* (see below, Bib.)
Turgenev	*CL* 281–82, 488; *SLC* 242
Twain	*P* 238
Van Vechten, Carl	*P* 361–63
Verga	*CL* 492; *P* 223–31, 240–50
Verlaine	*AA* 155; *CL* 21
Wells	*CL* 51, 54, 60, 203, 226, 278; *P* 346–50
White, Walter	*P* 361–63
Whitman	*CL* 257–58; *CP* 653; *P* 220–22, 319–20, 704–18; *S* 174–91; *SM* 230–40
Wilde	*CL* 1049; *F* 138; *P* 552, 752; *SM* 231–32
Williams, W. C.	*P* 334–36
Wordsworth	*AA* 155; *P* 23, 256; *R* 168–71; *SM* 202
Yeats	*CL* 47, 168; *SL* 86–87; *P* 307
Zola	*CB* 2 410; *P* 243

Bibliography

BOOKS BY LAWRENCE

Aaron's Rod (1922), London, Heinemann, 1950.

Apocalypse (1931), London, Secker, 1932.

"A Propos of Lady Chatterley's Lover," in *Sex, Literature and Censorship,* ed. H. T. Moore, New York, Twayne, 1953.

Assorted Articles (1930), London, Secker, 1932.

The Boy in the Bush, with M. L. Skinner, London, Secker, 1924.

The Collected Letters of D. H. Lawrence, ed. with intro. by H. T. Moore, 2 vols. New York, Viking Press, 1962.

The Complete Poems of D. H. Lawrence, ed. with intro. by Vivian de Sola Pinto and Warren Roberts, 2 vols. New York, Viking Press, 1964.

D. H. Lawrence: Selected Literary Criticism, ed. Anthony Beal, New York, Viking Press, 1956.

David (1926), London, Secker.

Etruscan Places (1932), New York, Viking Press, Compass Books, 1957.

The First Lady Chatterley (1944), New York, Dial Press, Berkley Edition, 1958.

Kangaroo (1923), London, Heinemann, 1950.

Lady Chatterley's Lover (1928), New York, Grove Press, 1959.

The Letters of D. H. Lawrence, ed. with intro. by Aldous Huxley, London, Heinemann, 1932.

Letters to Bertrand Russell, ed. H. T. Moore, New York, Gotham Book Mart, 1948.

Movements in European History (1921), pseud. Lawrence H. Davison, London, Oxford University Press.

Phoenix: The Posthumous Papers of D. H. Lawrence, ed. with intro. by Edward D. McDonald, London, Heinemann, 1936.

The Plumed Serpent (1926), London, Heinemann, 1950.

"The Portrait of M. M.," in *The Noble Savage* (New York, Meridian periodical, No. 2, 1960), pp. 178–253. Originally, preface to M. M. [Maurice Magnus] *Memoirs of the Foreign Legion,* 1924.

Psychoanalysis and the Unconscious and Fantasia of the Unconscious (1921–22), intro. by Philip Rieff, New York, Viking Press, Compass Books, 1960.

The Rainbow (1915), New York, Random House, Modern Library, 1943.

Reflections on the Death of a Porcupine and Other Essays (1925), London, Secker, 1934.

The Selected Letters of D. H. Lawrence, ed. with intro. by Diana Trilling, New York, Farrar, Straus and Cudahy, 1958.

Sons and Lovers (1913), New York, Viking Press, Compass Books, 1958.

Studies in Classic American Literature (1923), New York, Doubleday Anchor, 1953.

The Symbolic Meaning: The Uncollected Versions of Studies in Classic American Literature (1918–21), ed. Armin Arnold, New York, Viking Press, 1964.

The Tales of D. H. Lawrence, London, Secker, 1934.

Touch and Go, New York, Seltzer, 1920.

The Trespasser (1912), London, Heinemann, 1950.

Twilight in Italy (1916), London, Cape, 1929.

Women in Love (1920), New York, Viking Press, Compass Books, 1950.

WORKS ON LAWRENCE

Essays in books and periodicals and other books used in this study

Abrams, M. H., "The Correspondent Breeze: A Romantic Metaphor," in *English Romantic Poets: Modern Essays in Criticism,* ed. M. H. Abrams, New York, Oxford University Press, Galaxy, 1960.

——— The Mirror and the Lamp, New York, Oxford University Press, 1953.

Aldington, Richard, *Portrait of a Genius But. . . ,* London, Heinemann, 1950.

——— Introduction to *Selected Essays of D. H. Lawrence,* ed. R. Aldington, Baltimore, Penguin, 1954.

Arnold, Armin, *D. H. Lawrence and America,* New York, Philosophical Library, 1959.

Auden, W. H., "Some Notes on D. H. Lawrence," *The Nation* (April 26, 1947), pp. 482–84.

Blackmur, R. P., "D. H. Lawrence and Expressive Form," in his *Form and Value in Modern Poetry* (New York, Doubleday Anchor, 1957), pp. 253–67.

Bloom, Harold, "Lawrence, Blackmur, Eliot, and the Tortoise," in Moore, *A D. H. Lawrence Miscellany* (see below), pp. 360–69.

Bibliography

——— *Shelley's Mythmaking,* Yale Studies in English, 141, New Haven, Yale University Press, 1959.

——— *The Visionary Company: A Reading of English Romantic Poetry,* New York, Doubleday, 1961.

Brett, Dorothy, *Lawrence and Brett: A Friendship,* Philadelphia, Lippincott, 1933.

Brewster, Earl and Achsah, *D. H. Lawrence: Reminiscences and Correspondence,* London, Secker, 1934.

Brown, Norman O., *Life against Death,* New York, Random House, Modern Library paperback, 1959.

Bynner, Witter, *Journey with Genius: Recollections and Reflections concerning the D. H. Lawrences,* New York, John Day, 1951.

Carswell, Catherine, *The Savage Pilgrimage,* London, Secker, 1932.

Carter, Frederick, *D. H. Lawrence and the Body Mystical,* London, Archer, 1932.

Cary, Joyce, *Art and Reality,* London, Cambridge University Press, 1958.

Chambers, Jessie, *D. H. Lawrence: A Personal Record,* London, Cape, 1935.

Dahlberg, Edward, *Can These Bones Live,* New York, New Directions, 1960.

Deakin, William, "Lawrence's Attack on Joyce and Proust," *Essays in Criticism* (October 1957), pp. 383–403.

Eliade, Mircea, *The Myth of the Eternal Return,* trans. Willard Trask, New York, Pantheon, 1954.

Eliot, T. S., *After Strange Gods,* New York, Harcourt Brace, 1933.

——— Foreword to W. Tiverton's *D. H. Lawrence and Human Existence* (see below).

——— *The Sacred Wood* (1920), London, Methuen, 1945.

Feidelson, Charles, *Symbolism and American Literature,* Chicago, University of Chicago Press, 1953.

Fiedler, Leslie, *An End to Innocence,* Boston, Beacon Press, 1955.

——— *Love and Death in the American Novel,* New York, Criterion, 1960.

Foster, Richard, "Criticism as Poetry," *Criticism, 1,* No. 2 (1959), pp. 100–22.

——— "Criticism as Rage," in Moore, *A D. H. Lawrence Miscellany* (see below), pp. 312–25.

Fraser, G. S. *The Modern Writer and His World,* London, Derek Verschoyle, 1953.

Freeman, Mary, *D. H. Lawrence: A Basic Study of His Ideas,* Gainesville, University of Florida Press, 1955.

Freud, Sigmund, *Civilization and Its Discontents,* trans. Joan Riviere, New York, Doubleday Anchor, 1958.

Frye, Northrop, *Anatomy of Criticism,* Princeton, Princeton University Press, 1957.

——— *T. S. Eliot,* New York, Grove Press, 1963.

Goodheart, Eugene, *The Utopian Vision of D. H. Lawrence,* Chicago, University of Chicago Press, 1963.

Gurko, Leo, "Kangaroo: D. H. Lawrence in Transit," *Modern Fiction Studies, 10,* No. 4 (1964–65), 349–58.

Hoffman, F. J., and H. T. Moore, eds., *The Achievement of D. H. Lawrence,* Norman, University of Oklahoma Press, 1953.

Hough, Graham, *The Dark Sun: A Study of D. H. Lawrence,* New York, Macmillan, 1957.

Hulme, T. E., *Speculations* (1924), New York, Harcourt Brace, Harvest Book, 1962.

Huxley, Aldous, Introduction to *The Letters of D. H. Lawrence,* ed. A. Huxley, London, Heinemann, 1932.

Jung, C. G., *Modern Man in Search of a Soul,* Harcourt Brace, Harvest Book, 1954.

Kazin, Alfred, "The Function of Criticism Today," *Commentary, 30,* No. 5 (1960), pp. 369–78.

Kermode, Frank, *Romantic Image,* New York, Macmillan, 1957.

Klingopulos, G. D., Review of *D. H. Lawrence: Selected Literary Criticism,* in *Essays in Criticism* (July 1957), pp. 294–303.

Lawrence, Ada, and Stuart G. Gelder, *Young Lorenzo,* London, Secker, 1932.

Leavis, F. R., *For Continuity,* Cambridge, The Minority Press, 1931.

——— "Lawrence and Mr. Eliot," in Hoffman and Moore, *The Achievement of D. H. Lawrence* (see above), pp. 95–105.

——— *D. H. Lawrence: Novelist,* London, Chatto and Windus, 1955.

——— "The Wild Untutored Phoenix," in *The Importance of Scrutiny,* ed. with intro. by Eric Bentley (New York, Grove Press, 1948), pp. 338–43.

Lindenberger, Herbert, "Lawrence and the Romantic Tradition," in Moore, *A D. H. Lawrence Miscellany* (see below), pp. 326–41.

Luhan, Mabel Dodge, *Lorenzo in Taos,* New York, Knopf, 1932.

Mailer, Norman, *Advertisements for Myself,* New York, Putman, 1959.

Maud, Ralph, "D. H. Lawrence: True Emotion as Ethical Control in Art," *Western Humanities Review,* 9 (1955), 230–40.

Moore, Harry T., *The Intelligent Heart,* New York, Farrar, Straus, 1954.

——— ed., *A D. H. Lawrence Miscellany,* Carbondale, Southern Illinois University Press, 1959.

Bibliography

Moynahan, Julian, *The Deed of Life,* Princeton, Princeton University Press, 1963.

Mudrick, Marvin, "The Originality of The Rainbow," in Moore, *A D. H. Lawrence Miscellany* (see above), pp. 56–82.

Murry, Middleton, "D. H. Lawrence: Creative Iconoclast," in Moore, *A D. H. Lawrence Miscellany* (see above), pp. 3–6

———— *Reminiscences of D. H. Lawrence,* London, Cape, 1933.

———— *Son of Woman,* London, Cape, 1931.

Nehls, Edward, ed., *D. H. Lawrence: A Composite Biography,* 3 vols. Madison, University of Wisconsin Press, 1957–59.

Poggioli, Renato, *The Phoenix and the Spider,* Cambridge, Mass., Harvard University Press, 1957.

Rahv, Philip, "Criticism and Boredom," *New Statesman,* 56, No. 1434 (1958), pp. 310–12.

Rees, Richard, *Brave Men: A Study of D. H. Lawrence and Simone Weil,* Carbondale, Southern Illinois University Press, 1959.

Rieff, Philip, Introduction to D. H. Lawrence, *Psychoanalysis and the Unconscious and Fantasia of the Unconscious* (see above), 1960.

Shapiro, Karl, "The Unemployed Magician," in Moore, *A D. H. Lawrence Miscellany* (see above), pp. 378–95.

Simmons, Ernest, Introduction to F. Dostoevsky, *Crime and Punishment,* New York, Random House, Modern Library paperback, 1950.

Smith, Constance I., "A Note on Essays in Criticism," *Essays in Criticism* (July 1957), pp. 345–46.

Spilka, Mark, *The Love Ethic of D. H. Lawrence,* Bloomington, University of Indian Press, 1956.

Stevens, Wallace, *Opus Posthumous,* ed. Samuel French Morse, New York, Knopf, 1957.

Swinnerton, Frank, *The Georgian Literary Scene,* New York, Farrar and Rinehart, 1948.

Tedlock, E. W., *The Frieda Lawrence Collection of D. H. Lawrence Manuscripts,* Albuquerque, 1948.

Thoreau, H. D., *Walden,* intro. by Norman Holmes Pearson, New York, Rinehart, 1948.

Tindall, William York, *D. H. Lawrence and Susan His Cow,* New York, Columbia University Press, 1939.

Tiverton, William, *D. H. Lawrence and Human Existence,* New York, Philosophical Library, 1951.

Trilling, Diana, "Letter to a Young Critic," intro. to *The Selected Letters of D. H. Lawrence,* New York, Doubleday Anchor, 1961.

Trilling, Lionel, *The Liberal Imagination,* New York, Doubleday Anchor, 1957.

Turnell, Martin, "An Essay on Criticism," *Dublin Review,* 444 (1948), 72–95.

Vivante, Leone, *A Philosophy of Potentiality,* London, Routledge & Paul, 1955.

Vivas, Eliseo, *D. H. Lawrence: The Failure and the Triumph of Art,* Evanston, Northwestern University Press, 1960.

Widmer, Kingsley, *The Art of Perversity: D. H. Lawrence's Shorter Fictions,* Seattle, University of Washington Press, 1960.

———— "Our Demonic Heritage," in Moore, *A D. H. Lawrence Miscellany* (see above), pp. 13–27.

Index

(Works by Lawrence are listed alphabetically under Lawrence)

Abercrombie, Lascelles, 23–24
Abrams, M. H., 4n.
Action, temptation to, 109, 111, 131
Adams, Henry, 97
Aeschylus, 87. *See also* Greek culture, Orestes
Aesthetic theory, 41–74 passim
Aesthetic value vs. moral value, 3–4, 17–20, 24–27, 70–74, 79f., 82, 140–45, 148ff. passim. *See also* Art, and morality
After Strange Gods, quoted, 13
Aldington, Richard, 26–27, 32n.
Allegory, 48, 57–58
Americans, 15, 69, 119f., 121, 133–34, 140. *See also* Spirit of place
Anatomy of Criticism, 151
Angelico, Fra, 88n.
Anna Karenina, 8, 49, 73, 81–85, 90, 143–45. *See also* Tolstoi
Apocalyptic. *See* Modes, Visionary
Apuleius, 68
Aretino, Pietro, 26
Arnold, Armin, 1n., 12n., 128n., 135n.
Arnold, Matthew, 146, 151
Art: and life, 23f., 32, 45, 51–52, 56, 68–74, 88n., 148ff. passim; and morality, 40, 54–57, 62–74 passim. *See also* Aesthetic value
Attila, 89, 113
Auden, W. H., 12n.; quoted, 5, 46–47

Balzac, Honoré de, 49, 68
Baudelaire, Charles, 146; quoted, 5–6
Beethoven, Ludwig van, 15, 98n.
Being, 52. *See also* States of being
Bergson, Henri, 59
Berkeley, George, 60n.
Bible, 62, 69, 76, 87; Job, 91; Revelation, 66n.
Blackmur, R. P., quoted, 19, 44, 148
Blake, William, 10, 28–29, 34, 46, 50, 57, 62, 87, 89–90, 94–95, 106, 132n., 134, 146
Blood consciousness vs. mental consciousness, 7, 9–10, 15, 17–21, 44–45, 57n., 60, 62, 70, 76–77, 90, 105, 107, 132, 134 passim
Bloom, Harold, 12n.
Boccaccio, Giovanni, 66
Bolshevism, 71, 126f., 144. *See also* Russians
Botticelli, Sandro, 102
Bottom Dogs. See Dahlberg
Bourgeois consciousness, 52, 104, 132
Brontës, 105. See also *Jane Eyre*
Brothers Karamazov, 34ff., 92, 122. *See also* Dostoevsky
Brown, Norman O., 76n., 130
Bunyan, John: *Pilgrim's Progress,* 36; Mr. Facing-both-ways, 58
Burnet, John (*Early Greek Philosophy*), 32n.
Burns, Robert, 105
Burrow, Trigant, 42n.

Byron, Lord, 30–31

Calamus. See Whitman
Carter, Frederick, 70, 90n., 104n.
Cary, Joyce, 12n., 50–53, 63n.;
  quoted, 50–53 passim
Cassandra, 86
Cavalier poetry, 105
Cézanne, Paul, 106–07, 109, 119,
  125n.
Chambers, Jessie, quoted, 21n., 49,
  82n., 112n.
Chambers, May, quoted 21n.
Characterization, 70–74, 77ff., 82ff.
Chariot of the Sun. See Crosby
Charles I, 100
Chaucer, Geoffrey, 104–05
Chekhov, Anton, 78–79, 144–45
Christ, 36, 85, 88n., 92. *See also*
  Christianity, Jesus
Christianity, 15, 68–69, 80–82, 89,
  90n., 92, 97, 101ff., 110, 111, 121;
  Catholicism, 92, 113; Protestant-
  ism, 22n., 92, 110; Puritanism,
  130, 132, 133–34
Coleridge, S. T., 142
Comic. *See* Modes
Constant Nymph (Margaret Ken-
  nedy), 68
Convention, 52, 84, 113
Cooper, James Fenimore, 25, 39,
  83n., 119f., 126, 128, 133–34, 141.
  See also *Deerslayer,* Natty Bumppo
Correggio, 102
Courage, 6, 15, 17–20, 40
Craft, 36–40
Crèvecoeur, Michel de, 70, 128, 134
Crime and Punishment, 21n. *See also*
  Dostoevsky
Cromwell, Oliver, 100, 107f.
Crosby, Harry, 33n.
Crosland, Thomas W., 23
Cyclical view of history, 89, 94–95,
  97–110 passim
Cynicism, 68, 81, 116–17

Dahlberg, Edward, 116f., 118n., 133
Dana, Richard Henry, 136
Dante, 15, 65, 89, 102, 107, 125n.,
  147
David, 107
David Copperfield (Dora and Agnes),
  21n., 82n. *See also* Dickens
Davies, W. H., 26
Deakin, William, 12n.
Death, 14, 15, 76, 81–82, 89, 91,
  114ff., 130, 135 passim. *See also*
  Nullity
Death in Venice, 41, 116
Debussy, Claude, 102
Deerslayer, 83n., 110f., 126. *See also*
  Cooper, Natty Bumppo
Deledda, Grazia, 70
Democracy, 78, 89, 92, 101ff., 128,
  133–34, 139f.
Demonic. *See* Modes
Diabolism of modern woman, 90, 141
Dialectic, 8, 10, 90, 133
Dickens, 34. See also *David Copper-
  field*
Directness, Lawrence's, 34–36
Discipline, Lawrence's, 15, 33, 46
Disinterestedness, Lawrence's, 31–34
Don Juan, 77
Donne, John, 105, 110
Dos Passos, John, 27, 116f.
Dostoevsky, Fyodor, 20, 31, 34–37,
  40, 64, 78–79, 81, 92, 98n., 102,
  115, 124, 126, 136–37, 143–44.
  See also *Brothers Karamazov,
  Crime and Punishment, Idiot*
Drum Taps. See Whitman
Dürer, Albrecht, 102

Eliade, Mircea, 110
Eliot, George, 21n., 48. *See also* Maggie Tulliver, Hetty Sorrel
Eliot, T. S., 9, 12–14, 17, 27–28, 34,
  42–43, 68, 84, 93, 96, 97, 99,
  109f., 129, 135n., 141, 148, 150;
  quoted, 9, 13, 129

Emotion as cognitive and moral faculty, 3–4, 17–20, 43–45, 62, 65
Error, 5, 40, 77ff., 104, 111 passim; consolidation of, 134
Evil, 76f., 89–91 passim
Exclusive point of view, 5–6, 34, 149
Expressive form, 44, 65

Faerie Queene, 48, 134
Fall, myth of the, 59, 75–77, 97–110 passim, 111, 121, 124
Fallacy: affective, 94; intentional, 66
Feidelson, Charles, 10
Fiedler, Leslie, 12n., 33; quoted, 7
Fielding, Henry, 105
Flaubert, Gustav, 41–42, 78, 80, 102, 117
Flecker, J. E., 65
Form: of Lawrence's criticism, 2–4, 26; Lawrence's view of, 17, 39, 41–53, 57
Forster, E. M., 68, 69, 149
Foster, Richard, 12n., 52, 87n., 147; quoted 149–50
Fourth dimension, 54–57, 97n.
Franklin, Benjamin, 76n., 128
Fraser, G. S., 14
Frazer, James G., 32n.
Free verse, 65–66
Freud, Sigmund, 57n., 76, 91, 110
Frye, Northrop, 12n., 16, 51, 92; quoted, 96, 151

Galsworthy, John, 25–26, 39, 113
Gardiner, Rolf, 131
Garnett, Constance, 31n.
Garnett, Edward, 26, 31n., 40
Genre, 64f., 135, 142n.
Gibbon, Edward, 96
Gide, André, 68, 147
Gill, Eric, 39
Gissing, George, 26
Goethe, J. W., 76n., 102, 112, 146. *See also* Gretchen, Wilhelm Meister

Gourmont, Remy de, 24
Grahame, Cunninghame, 39
Gray, Thomas, 30–31
Grazzini, A. F., 21n.
Greek culture, 122–23; art, 119; drama, 71n., 79, 83–84, 105, 143; pre-Socratic philosophy, 16, 59, 89. *See also* Aeschylus, Homer, Plato, Sophocles
Gretchen (*Faust*), 83n.
Gurko, Leo, 47n.

Hamlet, 64, 79, 83, 87n., 100f., 104–05, 121, 131, 141. *See also* Shakespeare
Hamsun, Knut. See *Pan*
Hardy, Thomas, 34, 46, 52, 68–70, 81, 83–85, 91, 102, 115, 126. *See also* Jude, Sue Bridehead, Tess
Harrison, Jane (*Art and Ritual*), 32n.
Hawthorne, Nathaniel, 25, 83n., 115, 134. *See also* Hester Prynne, *Scarlet Letter*
Hazlitt, William, 43
Hegel, G. W. F., 87
Hemingway, Ernest, 27, 116f., 118n.
Heroines, 82n. *See also* Characterization
Hester Prynne, 83n., 90, 103, 141. *See also* Hawthorne, *Scarlet Letter*
Hetty Sorrel, 83n.
Hodgson, 38
Holy Ghost, 10, 59f., 101, 103–04, 144
Homer, 87n., 121ff.
Hough, Graham, 9, 93n.; quoted, 7, 51
Hulme, T. E., 97, 109, 148
Humanism, 16, 70f., 77–79, 96, 109, 124 passim
Husserl, Edmund, quoted, 50–51
Huxley, Aldous, 34, 40, 116f., 118n.; quoted, 9, 16

Ibsen, Henrik, 76n., 94, 125, 146
Idealism, 4, 15, 52–53, 61, 64, 76,

80, 89–90, 94, 128, 143n. passim.
See also Love ideal
Ideology, 51–52, 66f., 109; ideological literary criticism, 2, 7, 24–25, 65, 67, 73–74, 114ff., 133–45 passim, 150–52
Idiot, 34ff., 64, 102, 115. *See also* Dostoevsky
Idyllic. *See* Modes
If Winter Comes (Arthur Hutchinson), 68
Imagination, 20, 62, 106, 109
Immoralism, 68–69
In Our Time (Hemingway), 116f.
Independence, Lawrence's, 21–24
Indians (American), 127ff.
Individual authority, 13f., 17f., 27f., 33f., 83, 93, 149
Irony, 28, 43, 47, 68–69, 88

Jane Eyre, 66, 83n.
Jenner, Katherine (*Christ in Art*), 32n.
Jesus, 4, 53, 68, 86, 101, 107f., 111, 121, 139. *See also* Christ
Jews, 114
Job. *See* Bible
Johnson, Dr., 147, 151
Joyce, James, 42, 118f., 141, 145
Jude, 52, 90, 91. *See also* Hardy
Jung, C. G., 56–57, 59, 98n.

Kazin, Alfred, 12n., 149–50; quoted, 13, 146–47
Keats, John, 43, 55, 61–62, 65, 94n., 105
Kermode, Frank, 97–99; quoted, 97–98
Kierkegaard, S., 146
Klingopulos, G. D., 52
Koteliansky, S., 31n.

Lawrence, D. H., works by:
Aaron's Rod, 47, 91, 103, 127
Apocalypse, 3, 46, 92
"A Propos of Lady Chatterley's Lover," 92, 107, 123

Assorted Articles, 62
"Autobiographical Fragment" (*Phoenix*), 95n.
"Blind Man, The" (*Tales*), 47
"Blue Moccasins, The" (*Tales*), 91
"Borderline, The" (*Tales*), 95n.
Boy in the Bush, The, 17n., 91, 129
"Crown, The" (*Reflections*), 55, 89
"Daughters of the Vicar, The" (*Tales*), 83n.
David, 86n.
"Democracy" (*Phoenix*), 136, 139, 142n.
"Education of the People" (*Phoenix*), 15, 103
Etruscan Places, 92, 107, 123
Fantasia of the Unconscious, 60, 103
First Lady Chatterley, The, 127
"Fox, The" (*Tales*), 90
"Glad Ghosts" (*Tales*), 95n.
"Horse Dealer's Daughter, The" (*Tales*), 47
"Introduction to These Paintings" (*Phoenix*), 92, 100, 104–06
"John Galsworthy," 17–20
Kangaroo, 47n., 91, 129n.
Lady Chatterley's Lover, 25, 32, 47, 92, 94, 117, 118, 119, 123, 130
"Ladybird, The" (*Tales*), 10
"Last Laugh, The" (*Tales*), 95n.
Last Poems, 92
Lost Girl, The, 32
"Man Who Died, The" (*Tales*), 92, 95n., 107
"Morality and the Novel" (*Phoenix*), 54–55, 64
"Mother and Daughter" (*Tales*), 91
Movements in European History, 60
Nettles, 118n.
"Novel, The" (*Reflections*), 19n., 68–74, 87
Phoenix: The Posthumous Papers

of *D. H. Lawrence*, 1–2, 114n. passim
Plumed Serpent, The, 47, 91, 103, 118n., 129n.
"Pornography and Obscenity" (*Phoenix*), 129
"Preface" to Maurice Magnus' *Memoirs of the Foreign Legion*, 112f.
"Princess, The" (*Tales*), 90
Psychoanalysis and the Unconscious, 106
Rainbow, The, 47–48, 88, 92, 102–03, 123, 127
"Reality of Peace, The" (*Phoenix*), 114
"Rocking-Horse Winner, The" (*Tales*), 95n.
"St. Mawr" (*Tales*), 90
Sons and Lovers, 22n., 47, 49, 52, 86, 119
Studies in Classic American Literature, 1n., 2–3, 15, 28, 31, 64, 103, 119f., 128–29, 133–40 passim
Studies in Classic American Literature (earlier versions), 1n., 37n., 58–59, 103, 119, 127–29, 136–38 passim
"Study of Thomas Hardy" (*Phoenix*), 2, 22–23, 86–89, 99, 101f., 103 passim
"Surgery for the Novel—or a Bomb" (*Phoenix*), 69n.
"Things" (*Tales*), 61n., 91
Touch and Go., 91n.
Trespasser, The, 86, 98n.
Twilight in Italy, 100f., 103, 125
"Virgin and the Gypsy, The" (*Tales*), 59, 92
Women in Love, 41, 44, 45, 47–49, 61n., 71n., 91, 117n.
Lawrence, Frieda, 27n.
Leavis, F. R., 9, 12–14, 28, 31, 34, 48, 53, 130; quoted, 14, 28, 31
Lenin, 144. *See also* Bolshevism

Leonardo da Vinci, 15
Lewis, Wyndham, 97
Life, 3–4, 22, 53, 56, 58, 60, 68–72, 74, 89, 114ff. passim. *See also* Vitalism
Limits, 44–45, 136–37
Lindenberger, Herbert, 48
Literature of negation, 118f.
Literature of repudiation, 116–18
Lord Jim, 68
Love ideal, 52–53, 67–68, 115 passim. *See also* Idealism
Luhan, Mabel, 41n.

Macaulay, T. B., 18
McDonald, Edward, quoted, 130
Maggie Tulliver, 21n., 83n. *See also* Eliot
Magnus, Maurice, 112, 116f.
Mailer, Norman, 12n., 51–53, 63n., 91n., 151; quoted, 53, 63n., 91n.
Main Street, 68
Mallarmé, Stéphane, 102
Malvolio, 94
Manly love, 119f., 137f., 141
Mann, Thomas, 41, 116
Mansfield, Katherine, 27n., 34, 126
Marsh, Edward, 38
Marx, Karl, 76, 144, 146, 151
Mastro-don Gesualdo, 121–23. *See also* Verga
Maud, Ralph, 12n., 14; quoted, 7
Maupassant, Guy de, 126
Melville, Herman, 59, 70, 80, 115, 124, 134, 136, 142. See also *Moby Dick*
Mental consciousness. *See* Blood consciousness
Metaphor, Lawrence's, 9–11, 59, 61–62. *See also* Symbolism
Metrical verse, 65, 94n.
Michelangelo, 102, 107, 125n.
Middle Ages, 96, 100ff., 112–14
Miller, Henry, 151
Milton, John, 52, 89, 98, 132, 147

Miscellany, A D. H. Lawrence, 149n. passim
Moby Dick, 28, 58, 134, 142. *See also* Melville
Modes, 93–95; apocalyptic, 51, 87f., 91–94, 104, 124; comic, 93f.; demonic, 77, 90–93, 134; idyllic, 91–92, 123; rhapsodic, 93n.; tragic, 75–95 passim
Molière, 93–94
Moore, Harry T., 2n.
Moral earnestness, 5–6, 39–40, 59, 80, 95 passim
Morality of nature, 53, 84f. passim. *See also* Vitalism
Morris, Wright, 151
Mozart, W. A., 146
Murry, Middleton, 27n., 31n., 34, 131, 138; quoted, 151
Myth, 7–8, 57–59, 95, 97–110 passim, 120

Naïveté, 43, 57n., 71, 77
Napoleon, 112
Natty Bumppo, 126, 128. *See also* Cooper, *Deerslayer*
Naturalism vs. supernaturalism, 55–56, 95n.
Nerval, Gérard de, 97n.
Nietzsche, Friedrich, 32n., 53, 60, 94–95, 101, 146, 151
Noah, 113
Novel, Lawrence's theory of, 46ff., 62–74
Nullity, 81, 89–90, 103, 114. *See also* Death

Odyssey, 121ff.
Oedipus, 83, 105
Orestes, 100

Painting: English, 104–07; French, 104–07; Lawrence's, 27n.
Pamela, 66n.
Pan (Knut Hamsun), 68
Permanence, 54–57, 98n.

Personality vs. impersonality, 41ff., 78, 106f., 123–24, 126. *See also* Emotion
Petronius, 26
Phallic consciousness, 7, 22, 69, 119, 121, 129
Pickthall, Marmaduke, 39
Pity, 78–80, 98n., 122. *See also* Tragedy
Plato, 4, 52, 53, 56, 86, 102, 107f., 111
Poe, E. A., 37, 115f., 134, 141–42, 143n.
Point Counter Point, 116f. *See also* Huxley
Pope, Alexander, 41
Popular art, 68–69, 131
Potentiality, 50–53, 110, 124
Pound, Ezra, 7n., 97, 147
Practical critic, Lawrence as, 37–39
Prophetic: Function of artist, 111–12; intention of own work, 53, 97ff., 102f., 106, 121, 140; interpretation of other work, 3, 100ff., 115, 119, 127, 131f., 133f., 143f. *See also* Visionary
Proust, Marcel, 118f., 141f., 146
Psychoanalysis, 143n. *See also* Freud
Psychologist, Lawrence as. *See* Blood consciousness, Emotion, Unconscious
Puritanism. *See* Christianity

Radical innocence, 76f., 80, 152
Raphael, 11, 102, 110, 125
Realism, 48–49, 64, 78
Rebirth, 47, 114ff., 119ff., 133, 136 passim
Reductiveness of Lawrence's criticism, 5–8
Rees, Richard, 6, 150n.
Relationship, 3–4, 43–44, 53–55, 60–61, 70–72, 78, 101, 103, 119f. passim
Rembrandt, 102, 106

Index

Renaissance, 96, 100–10, 119, 125, 127f.
Restoration, 105
Resurrection, 71. *See also* Tolstoi
Revelation. *See* Bible
Richardson, Samuel. See *Pamela*
Romanticism: aesthetic of, compared to Lawrence's, 43–44; demonism of, 90; fusion with realism 48n.; image of correspondent breeze in poetry of, 4n.; impressionism, 24; irony, 43; Lawrence as modern romatic, 149–52; Lawrence's antagonism to, 32n.; and modernism, 146–47; mythmaking in, 97–99; nostalgia in, 112; poetry of, Lawrence's love for, 65; psychology of, compared to Lawrence's, 61–62; reconciliation of opposites in, 14–16; relation of art and life in, 87–88; vs. Hulme, 109–10
Russians, 78–79, 81, 121–23, 144. *See also* Bolshevism, Spirit of place

St. Paul, 89, 111, 140
Sainte-Beuve, C. A., 18, 46
Sartre, Jean Paul, 60
Satan, 89–90, 132
Scarlet Letter, 76–77, 103, 141, 143n. *See also* Hawthorne, Hester Pynne
Schiller, J. C. F. von, 146
Scholarship, Lawrence's attitude toward, 18, 20n., 22
Self-awareness, 19, 25–34, 148
Self-consciousness, 19, 28–34, 42–43, 78, 98, 102, 108, 121ff., 130
Sensationalism, 115f., 143n.
Sentimentalism, 68, 81, 114, 116f.
Shakespeare, 38, 52, 65, 71n., 79, 82n., 83–84, 87n., 100f., 102, 104–05, 107, 112, 131. *See also* Hamlet, Malvolio
Shapiro, Karl, quoted, 29n.
Shaw, George Bernard, 32n., 90, 94, 110, 113, 146, 147
Shelley, P. B., 65, 94, 102, 105, 132n.

Sherman, Stuart, 39
Shestov, Leo, 39, 119, 120f.
Sincerity, 6, 17–20; risks of, 27–29, 52
Skinner, Mollie, 17n.
Smith, Constance, quoted, 73
Social consciousness, 44, 47, 69, 71n., 76–77, 82ff., 125 passim. *See also* Blood consciousness
Social critic, Lawrence as, 130–32 passim
Song of Myself. See Whitman
Sophocles, 87n.
Soul, 3–4, 13, 17–24, 27, 28, 59f., 135–36 passim
Spilka, Mark, 86n.
Spirit of place, 124–29, 133–34; America, 124, 127–29, 138ff.; Australia, 129; Germany, 125; Italy, 125; Mexico, 129; northern vs. southern Europe, 121ff.; Russia, 126–27
Spontaneity, 6, 14f., 42, 57n., 71 passim. *See also* Potentiality, Vitalism
Spoon River Anthology, 26
Sportsman's Sketches, 126. *See also* Turgenev
Standards, 3–4, 18, 22–24
States of being, 46–49, 52
Sterne, 105
Stevens, Wallace, 50–51
Strindberg, August, 21, 125
Style: of Lawrence's criticism, 8–11, 101–02, 123; Lawrence's view of, 17, 39, 41–42
Subjectivity, 9–10, 19–20, 22–24, 61f., 125, 141, 148
Sue Bridehead, 52, 86, 90, 102. *See also* Hardy
Swift, Jonathan, 105, 147
Swinburne, A. C., 38
Swinnerton, Frank, quoted, 31n.
Sylvestre Bonnard, 68
Symbolism, 10, 48f., 50, 56–62, 108. *See also* Metaphor

Index

Tact, Lawrence's, 27–29
Taste, Lawrence's, 24–27
Taylor, Rachel Annand, 38
Tchekov. *See* Chekhov
Tess, 82n., 83–85. *See also* Hardy
Thoreau, H. D., 147; quoted, 112
Tindall, William York, 148
Titian, 106
Tiverton, William, 42–43, 60n.
Tolstoi, Leo, 2n., 28, 69–73, 81–85, 102, 115, 119, 126, 143–45. See also *Anna Karenina, Resurrection, War and Peace*
Tone, Lawrence's, 5–8, 31, 73
Tradition, 44, 113; traditional form, 44, 47, 49
Tragedy, 49–50, 68, 75–95 passim
Tragic. *See* Modes
Transvaluation of values, 52–53
Trilling, Diana, quoted, 27n.
Trilling, Lionel, 12n.; quoted, 42n.
Turgenev, Ivan, 83n., 126
Turnell, Martin, 5, 12n., 149–50; quoted, 8, 24
Turner, William, 11, 102

Ulysses, 68. *See also* Joyce
Unconscious, 9–10, 17–21, 51, 76
Unconscious intention, 3, 25, 27, 32, 37n., 66–74, 75, 128, 131, 133–35, 142–43 passim. *See also* Blood consciousness, Soul

Van Gogh, Vincent, 54, 88n., 97n.
Van Vechten, Carl, 27
Velasquez, 106

Verga, Giovanni, 37, 69–70, 82, 121–24
Visionary, 75, 82, 87–88, 92, 95, 112, 120. *See also* Modes, apocalyptic; Prophetic function of artist
Vitalism, 50–53, 57, 59, 81, 94
Vivante, Leone, 12n., 50–53; quoted, 4n., 31n., 50–53 passim, 66
Vivas, Eliseo, quoted, 48–49, 59n.
Voltaire, 147

Wagner, Richard, 146
War and Peace, 71–72. *See also* Tolstoi
Wells, H. G., 23–24, 118n.
White consciousness, 115, 133ff.
White, Walter, 27
Whitman, 7, 15, 29–31, 65–66, 76n., 80, 94n., 115, 119f., 125n., 133–42
Widmer, Kingsley, 12n., 14; quoted, 90
Wilde, Oscar, 52, 76n.
Wilhelm Meister, 77. *See also* Goethe
Wilkinson, Walter, 31–32, 39
Will, 52–53, 75–77, 80, 119f., 127 passim
Williams, Tennessee, 151
Williams, W. C., 29n., 39
Wilson, Edmund, 12n.
Wordsworth, William, 61–62, 102, 105, 146
World of William Clissold, 118n. *See also* Wells
World War I, 143n.

Yeats, W. B., 26, 94–95, 97–99, 101, 108, 109f., 134; quoted, 112